# Carving Architectural Detail in Wood

## The Classical Tradition

# CARVING ARCHITECTURAL DETAIL IN WOOD

## THE CLASSICAL TRADITION

FREDERICK WILBUR

*Frederick Wilbur*

GUILD OF MASTER CRAFTSMAN PUBLICATIONS LTD

First published 2000 by
Guild of Master Craftsman Publications Ltd
Castle Place, 166 High Street, Lewes, East Sussex BN7 1XU

Reprinted 2002, 2003

ISBN 1 86108 158 8

Edited by Stephen Haynes
Designed by Ian Hunt Design
Cover by Graham Willmott, GMC Publications design studio
Engraving from Palladio's Four Books of Architecture by courtesy of
Dover Publications, Inc.; photograph of doorway by courtesy of
the Hammond–Harwood House Association, Annapolis, MD

Set in Stempel Schneidler, Monotype Castellar and Futura Book
Colour origination by Viscan Graphics (Singapore)
Printed and bound by Kyodo Printing, (Singapore)

# SAFETY

Woodcarving should not be a dangerous activity, provided that sensible precautions are taken to avoid unnecessary risk.

● Always ensure that work is securely held in a suitable clamp or other device, and that workplace lighting is adequate.

● Keep tools sharp; blunt tools are dangerous because they require more pressure and may behave unpredictably. Store them so that you, and others, cannot touch their cutting edges accidentally.

● Be particular about disposing of shavings, finishing materials, oily rags, etc., which may be a fire hazard.

● Do not work when your concentration is impaired by drugs, alcohol, or fatigue.

● Do not remove safety guards from power tools; pay attention to electrical safety.

● The safety advice in this book is intended for your guidance, but cannot cover every eventuality: the safe use of hand and power tools is the responsibility of the user. If you are unhappy with a particular technique or procedure, do not use it—there is always another way.

## MEASUREMENTS

Although care has been taken to ensure that metric measurements are true and accurate, they are only conversions from imperial; they have been rounded up or down to the nearest whole millimeter, or to the nearest convenient equivalent in cases where the imperial measurements themselves are only approximate. When following the projects, use either the metric or the imperial measurements; do not mix units.

*This book is dedicated to my father,*
*Robert L. Wilbur (1915–1998),*
*and to my mother,*
*Martha M. Wilbur,*
*who encouraged me to pursue my academic*
*as well as my artistic interests*

# ACKNOWLEDGMENTS

I must express an incalculable debt to all my woodcarving predecessors, both known and unknown, whose work has inspired and taught me and has contributed to the enduring tradition of classical woodcarving. I feel fortunate here to be adding to this tradition.

The credit for this work should be shared with many others, but first among them is my wife Elizabeth, who tolerated the mess, who proofread over and over, who encouraged me during all the years of wood chips. Without her this endeavor would not have come to fruition.

I would like especially to thank Edward A. Chappell, Director of Architectural Research, Colonial Williamsburg Foundation, for his unfailing encouragement and for facilitating arrangements with others at Colonial Williamsburg: Roberta G. Laynor, Architectural Conservator and Keeper of the Francis H. Lenygon Collection of Architectural Fragments; Ronald L. Hurst, Vice-President for Collections; and Catherine H. Grosfils, Visual Resources Editorial Librarian at the Rockefeller Library of the Colonial Williamsburg Foundation.

I would also like to thank sincerely Stephen Haynes, my editor, for his sensitive questioning, his good humor, and his tolerance of my constant revisions; and Stephanie Horner, Senior Managing Editor at GMC Publications, must be thanked for her unfailing understanding and support in the complicated process of producing this book.

Mrs James C. Wheat must be thanked for graciously allowing me to take photographs of the work I and others did for Blandfield, Caret, VA.

## THANKS ALSO TO:

Phillip Beaurline for photographing the mantelpiece

The British Museum, London, for permission to use my photographs of pieces in the museum

Thomas A. Goddard for permitting me to photograph several picture frames in his collection

John Grafton of Dover Publications, Inc. for the use of material from several of their publications

Melissa Heaver, Director of Museum Collections, National Trust for Historic Preservation, for permission to use my photographs of Drayton Hall, Charleston, SC

Mr and Mrs George M. Kaufman for the use of the photographs of the Philadelphia desk and bookcase

John Lavine, Editor of *Woodwork*, and Ross Periodicals for use of an article of my authorship (#54, December 1998)

Diane and Howie Long and Jimmy Pickel, Sr for permitting photography in their homes

Maria Mauzy and Jan Jordan of the American School of Classical Studies at Athens for photographs of Greek temples

The Royal Institute of British Architects for use of the molding comparison from Sir Banister Fletcher's *History of Architecture*

Charles J. Stick, who designed the gatepost and supplied photographs of it

Frederica Struse of the Hammond–Harwood House, Annapolis, MD for permitting photographs of the interior

The Victoria and Albert Museum, London, for permission to use my photographs of pieces in the museum

Professor Carroll W. Westfall, Dean, School of Architecture, Notre Dame University, for the use of his photograph of Palladio's Villa Almerico

Mrs Robert L. Wilbur for photographs of furniture in her home.

# CONTENTS

# NOTES TO THE READER

## Overview of architectural carving • Tools and techniques

This book illustrates and explains the designs and methods of carving classical architectural ornament, their abundant variations, and their appropriate uses in architectural spaces and in their adaptation to furniture. Because architectural elements are more often than not part of a larger project involving communication between architect, millwork (joinery) company, and carver, one major aim of this book is to clarify the terms which serve as common ground among them. It should be pointed out that the furniture maker, interior designer, and other allied trades such as framer/gilder and restorer can benefit from the information presented here, because so much architectural ornament has been adapted to their respective endeavors.

Architectural carving in many respects is set apart from the usual notion of the bearded whittler rocking on the front porch producing diminutive figure sculptures. It has a breadth of application which encompasses all the techniques of the art of woodcarving, from custom-made millwork to high-relief realism as developed by Grinling Gibbons. In most architectural work there is a balance between the geometric precision required in producing multiple elements and the artistic vivacity which endows the work with a life of its own. We shall see that a broad sweep of knowledge is required to produce the elements which distinguish architectural styles, though Edith Wharton, in *The Decoration of Houses* (p. 11), lamented that "Unfortunately, it is usually by ornamental details, rather than by proportion, that people distinguish one style from another."

The critic might point out that architectural carving is of a lesser stature when compared to the art of sculpture—that the architectural carver is a copyist, and is satisfied with repetitive tasks—but this is a simplistic observation. A comprehensive understanding and uncommon skill are necessary to balance the many aspects of the work; not only to execute the work accurately, but to do so efficiently enough to make a living. There is little point in elevating one genre of carving above another, stating that one is "better" than another, because each has its own purpose, its own story or process, and its own particular attraction. To say that limewood floral carving is superior to egg-and-dart molding, or that a floral rosette is a higher level of achievement than a duck decoy, is nonsense.

The only useful comparisons are within genres, and even here only levels of expertise or sophistication can be considered. And the degree of sophistication in the work may be varied by the carver for many reasons: to suit the purpose, character, or ambiance of the work, its location, changing light, and not least, the client's budget.

This book emphasizes the practical side of fabricating historically accurate carved architectural elements, and avoids academic theory—though admittedly the first chapter attempts an overview of historical precedent and addresses Edith Wharton's lament. Each chapter deals with a specific architectural element or motif which traditionally lends itself to decoration. Beginning with descriptions and definitions, the carving of that element is then explained, relying on drawings and photographs for clarification of the text. Each chapter includes a number of photographs of finished examples which illustrate the context in which that element is used. Some show work in stone or other materials, but in every case they have been chosen to illustrate what can be carved in wood.

To tie the various elements together and bring them closer to hand, the last chapter presents several projects—mantelpieces, gateposts, picture frames—in photographs and drawings. To make the book as helpful as possible, there is also a Glossary of all the

> *Wood carving calls for the exercise of manual skill and artistic feeling. Both of these are essential to the production of any good piece of carved work. Manual skill comes from the knowledge of the shapes and uses of tools and by putting this knowledge into actual practice. Artistic feeling is largely instinctive, but it can also be inculcated and developed. Thus almost anyone with strength and eyesight can learn to carve...*
>
> PAUL HASLUCK

terms printed in bold type in the text, and a Select Bibliography with some appropriate notes. There are generous margins for those who read with a pencil in hand.

A complete understanding of the forms of ornamentation presented here will equip the carver to produce all the primary elements required for the decoration of classical architecture. Certainly there are many more examples which could have been included if space were not an issue, but there is enough here for a competent execution of the orders of architecture to be accomplished. This book, regrettably, cannot address free-standing and high-relief sculpture, which on some buildings relegates decorative carving to a subservient role. It is not meant to be an academic history of ornament, nor an exhaustive exploration of all possible variations, but an introduction to the field of carving woodwork and a guide to carving classical and classically derived decoration. The demonstrations are of the simpler versions; I hope to have the opportunity in a later book to explore some of these elements in their more complex incarnations.

## WORKSPACE AND WORKING METHODS

One of the most important tools the carver can possess is a well-stocked library, either personal or public. As you will find, there have been numerous histories and pattern books published over the centuries, beginning with Vitruvius and continuing today with the many successful periodicals on period details, restoration, and adaptation of classical details to modern life. I have drawn attention in the Select Bibliography to those which I consider essential. There is no substitute for personal research: collecting photographs from catalogues, magazines, and other sources, and taking drawing courses at the community college. You should also document your own work in photographs and drawings.

One does not usually think of one's workspace as a tool, but it certainly will influence your work. Efforts should be made to provide adequate space, efficiently laid out and with plenty of light. In my instructions I assume that proper equipment is available; further advice can be found in several publications listed in the Bibliography.

Ideally, natural light is best for the studio or workspace, but it should be diffuse light. Painting walls and ceiling white is one way to achieve this, regardless of the light source. Fluorescent lighting is economical and, though color balances vary, provides even light.

If possible, have different groups of lights on separate switches so that the direction of light can be controlled to some extent. A strong raking light will show irregularities, but will also create deep shadows which may disguise them. It is logical that when carving a symmetrical design the lighting should be evenly distributed over the work as it proceeds, so that the shadows created by the work are also symmetrical. Therefore, the lighting should be either extremely diffuse or directly perpendicular to the workpiece. It is always a good idea to inspect your work in different lights, or by turning or tipping the work in a strong light. Simply turning off the electric light (if there are any windows at all) or taking the work outside into the sunlight will show up scratches, fuzz, and other blemishes.

It is hard to realize that one's habits may not be the best to accomplish the task at hand. Everyone works in his or her own way, but it is generally accepted that much time can be lost looking for tools or moving material from a workspace only to put them back after the space has been temporarily used for a different operation. Much time is also wasted if you have to resand or recarve an area because poor light disguised some flaw. Arranging the workshop in the same way as a kitchen, making use of a triangular layout, can save much time and fatigue. The three key areas—tool storage, working surface, and sharpening area—should be in close proximity to one another. Ideally, the bench should be an island in the workroom so that access to the carving is flexible and large projects can be easily accommodated. The sharpening station should be off one end of the bench so that from either side it is not more than a step or two away. A place for permanent storage of carving tools is a wise idea, because this keeps them better protected while other operations are being performed. Managing your tools efficiently will save time; only the tools needed for a particular project should occupy the bench.

## TOOLS AND TECHNIQUES

I have assumed that the reader who is willing to persevere through a substantial architectural project already has the basic knowledge and equipment for such an undertaking. There are numerous publications on these subjects, particularly Chris Pye's definitive *Woodcarving Tools, Materials & Equipment* (GMC Publications, 1994). I generally agree with his recommendations for a "starter kit", but would advise two things.

Firstly, begin your purchases with a range of sweeps of the straight-shanked pattern, avoiding the special-situation tools such as longbent, frontbent, or backbent tools, which are more difficult to use and are not used as often. For instance, purchase a shallow-sweep gouge such as a #2 or #3 in ¾in (20mm) size, because this is used to smooth the background of relief carvings and large plain surfaces; turned over, it rounds convex surfaces nicely. The flatter sweeps tend to be more versatile than quicker sweeps, both for setting in and for modeling. Gouges of #5 and #7 sweep, about ½–¾in (14–20mm) wide, are extremely useful in setting in and modeling foliage, giving it the proper curve and flow. A #8 of ⅜–½in (10–14mm) is necessary for deep recesses such as flutes, being a little less than a semicircle in sweep. For bosting in, preparing to set in around a relief, as well as for veining, a #11 of ¼–⅜in (6–10mm) is also recommended. There are many occasions when we need to incise lines or V-grooves, either as design elements or as preliminary guidelines, so a ⅜in (10mm) #12, which is a parting tool with a 60° angle, is handy. Add to your collection by purchasing these gouges in a range of sizes, accumulating the extremes as needed. (The tool numbering adopted in this book is that used by the Swiss brand Pfeil. Actual sweeps vary somewhat within and among manufacturers' lists, so comparisons are difficult; it is the relative shallowness or quickness of the sweep which is important.)

Secondly, realize that unique situations will require a specific tool—this is particularly true when trying to reproduce an existing piece—so that obtaining tools is a career-long process. The various manufacturers or their retailers often carry only particular sweeps out of the dozens possible, and it is not necessarily advantageous to buy all of one brand of tool. Please refer to the Select Bibliography for other books which contain chapters on tools and sharpening.

In this book, tools and equipment will be specified only as far as is necessary for the task being described. For example, when a deep cut is required an appropriately "quick" or deeply swept gouge will be suggested, but not a specific size. There are several reasons for this. One of the points of this book is to show many alternative possibilities for a design, allowing the reader to adapt and discover. Further, you may not have the particular gouge which is recommended, in which case you must design your project around the available selection of tools. I also do not expect you to read or work straight through the book, but to use it as a resource which can help you achieve your desire to enhance a specific project.

# MATERIALS

Much architectural work is painted or finished in some way so as to obscure the grain; this allows the viewer to notice the play of light and shadow on the forms instead of being distracted by the natural interest of the wood. House-trim moldings are often painted white to enhance the shadows. Strong grain confuses the eye and obscures the form. Bland, straight-grained wood is preferred, therefore, on aesthetic grounds—and on practical grounds as well, because such material is more easily carved. It must be said that if one is attempting to replicate a particular style it is probably a good idea to use the wood associated with that style. For instance, Gothic church work is chiefly in oak, while eighteenth-century furniture is predominantly mahogany and walnut. There are exceptions to this (I have myself carved linenfold panels in mahogany and claw-and-ball feet in oak), and part of the evolution of ornament is to introduce iconoclastic notions to the mainstream.

The following list of woods is an expression of personal preference, though anyone working to commission may not have the luxury of choice. This list does not take into consideration environmental, sociopolitical, or economic concerns. I have carved a variety of woods including shedua, sassafrass, Engelmann spruce, heart pine, koa, and dogwood. But when there is a choice, the primary concern is suitability to the required task. For instance, basswood is an unwise choice for door architraves, as it is too soft for constant wear; while the grain of red oak obscures the perception of fine detail. Generally, the finer and tighter the grain, the better for obtaining detail. Light-colored woods tend to show shadow, and therefore carved forms, better than dark ones—but this depends on the depth of relief and on the lighting.

Basswood, *Tilia americana*
Black cherry, *Prunus serotina*
Black walnut, *Juglans nigra*, and butternut, *J. cinerea*
Eastern white pine, *Pinus strobus*
Jelutong, *Dyera costulata*
Mahogany, *Swietenia mahogani*
Red maple, *Acer rubrum*, and silver maple, *A. saccharinum*
Sugar pine, *Pinus lambertiana*
White oak, *Quercus alba*, and northern red oak, *Q. rubra*
Yellow poplar (tulip tree), *Liriodendron tulipifera*

My list is of course confined to timbers readily available in North America. European readers will be able to substitute closely related species, such as lime or linden (*Tilia* x *europaea*) for basswood, sycamore (*Acer pseudoplatanus*) for the maples, or English oak (*Quercus robur*) for white or red oak; readers elsewhere will have to rely on their knowledge of the timbers available to them.

Another material that should be mentioned is high-density urethane foam (oh horrors!), which comes in 8 x 4ft (2.4 x 1.2m) sheets and in various densities and thicknesses. It is a viable material for exterior work; sign makers use it extensively for three-dimensional graphics. It does not degrade, especially when primed and painted, and it does not take on water, thereby expanding and contracting. It is expensive, and nasty stuff to work, as the dust takes on an electrical charge and sticks to everything. It readily dulls carving tools, so as far as possible it should be machined; roughing out can be done with rotary cutters. Finally, as I grow older, I shudder to think of the health risks from inhaling the very fine dust.

It must be pointed out that much architectural ornament was and is made of other materials such as terracotta, plaster, composition, stamped metal, extruded plastic, and so forth. Much wooden ornament today is made by computer-directed routers and pressing machines. These products all have their place in the larger picture, and to disparage them is narrow-minded, but often they are not accurate copies of classical ornamentation and must be used with caution.

In the techniques about to be explained there is no "right" or "wrong" way: what we must aim to achieve is more efficient habits with fewer adverse consequences. Carvers may use their tools in any way they like, but knowing the consequences of their actions allows them to avoid breaking the tool, severing their thumb, or becoming frustrated and discouraged.

There is nothing arcane or mysterious about architectural carving, though there is a plethora of tools and terms to mystify the uninitiated. The secret lies in simply knowing the order in which things are done—as David Esterly has so admirably explained in his recent study of the work of Grinling Gibbons. One should cultivate one's confidence and strive for clarity, crispness, workmanship with purpose and resolve. As James Krenov states in *The Fine Art of Cabinetmaking* (p. 6), "Without a certain attitude to our craft, information is of little value."

# A PERSONAL NOTE

I am sympathetic to imperfection—it has value—and see myself always as an apprentice to my work. I believe in the integrity of being self-taught. Of course the artisan is always striving for excellence of expression, but endemic to the nature of craftsmanship is the unsatisfactoriness of the creative act, which must always include on some level experiment and chance. Each piece of handwork embodies a story, a tale of process. The unique quality of handwork makes possible the complex sense of exhilaration and pride in achievement that all art strives to communicate. There should be no attempt to imitate the work accomplished by machine or computer—though I hesitate to romanticize working with a once-living material. Things of quality take time—not only in the sense of a long-enduring tradition, but also in the simple sense that handwork includes the idea of mindfulness.

# A NOTE ON TERMINOLOGY

Throughout the present work the following terms have consistently been used as defined below:

**blank** a piece of material which has been shaped by hand or machine to the dimensions of the element to be made, such as a lathe-turned rosette, shaper-run molding, or the complex curves of a Corinthian capital produced by large gouges and files.

**design** the two-dimensional drawing or **cartoon** of the ornament to be made.

**grounding** the background: either the recessed part of the blank, or the surface upon which the ornamentation is applied.

**layout** the process of using the pattern, as well as other guidelines, to define the shape of the element on the blank.

**modeling** the surface treatment carried out after the outline of the ornamentation has been defined.

**pattern** any means of transferring the design to the material, such as a photocopied drawing glued onto the blank, a tracing, or a metal template.

**profile** the sectional shape of an element—usually in referring to moldings which have been cut with shaped cutters.

CHAPTER

# CLASSICAL DESIGN

Historical notes • Proportion • The orders • Designing for carving

Traditional architectural carving requires familiarity with a number of fields, each of which contributes to the success of the carved work. The need for a practical knowledge of building construction, joinery, wood species, tools, and equipment is obvious. Beyond these immediate concerns, it is essential that the aspiring architectural carver be well versed in architectural history and the history of ornament. Mathematics, particularly geometry, is involved in many aspects of classical architecture. A curiosity for the natural world, from an aesthetic as well as a scientific perspective, is also necessary. "The Greeks, who gave a lot of attention and thought to their works of art, used the same word for both art and craft, namely *techne*" (Demetri Porphyrios, *Classical Architecture*, p. 29).

The ornamentation of buildings has, no doubt, a primal beginning, evolving through advances in technology, the ebb and flow of cultural history, and periods of popularity and disuse. Classical architecture, though susceptible to these vagaries, has continued to survive. It is not merely a *style*, as styles are most often associated with a specific period of time or a particular designer; for example, we speak of the Adam style, Baroque, or Mannerism. Classical architecture has a broad vocabulary that is surprisingly free of theory and abstraction. The carver should use the momentum of this large body of cultural consciousness as a valuable resource, and consider it as the framework in which he practices his craft. Integrating ornamentation into the larger structural composition is the mark of an accomplished carver who understands the essence of classical design.

> *On the artistic side, an appreciation of form, proportion, and balance is essential—in fact, it is true to say that no excellence of technique can make up for lack of artistic expression.*
>
> WILLIAM WHEELER

The phrase "Classical Tradition", as used in the title of this book, refers to the structures and ornamentation of ancient Greece and Rome; but it also encompasses the long tradition derived from these two civilizations, whose subdivisions have titles such as Renaissance, Palladianism, and Greek Revival. We speak of the "classical" period of a culture as a time when the various aspects of that culture coalesce into a stunning expression of human endeavor. We speak of classical music, classic films, literary classics, and bestow on them the status of an enduring standard, an authoritative example of artistic heritage. There have been many classical traditions around the world, but the influence of Greek and Roman civilization on Western culture cannot be overstated. The few paragraphs which follow cannot do the subject justice; please refer to the Select Bibliography for further reading.

Greek and Roman architecture and its derivatives are based on mathematical proportion, which is evident in floor plans, elevations, and therefore volumes. Though the usual touchstone for exploring classicism is a discussion of the "orders" of architecture, the essence of the idea is the more general use of symmetry and proportion. These principles pertain to the whole structure and not merely to the columns propping up the façade. The essence of classical design is the all-embracing idea that measurement, and therefore form and numbers, should attempt to replicate the perfection of Nature. There is no generic Egyptian temple or typical Gothic church in the same way that there is a definite image or entity of the Greek temple. This is true because the latter has a constant range of elements and relationships, both in kind and in number, which give it an internal consistency and coherence. The basis of classical architecture is composition: the relationship of parts to wholes, and vice versa, in a way that combines freedom with formality. Consequently, classical architecture places more emphasis on form than meaning, values technical precision over emotional ambiguity and restraint over uncontrolled extravagance.

For the present-day carver, the point of learning about the classical tradition is to become familiar with the accepted scheme of ornamentation and what is or is not appropriate for a given use. Even Vitruvius, writing in the first century BCE, complained that

those subjects which were copied from actual realities are scorned in these days of bad taste. . . . For how is it possible that a reed should really support a roof, or a candelabrum a pediment with its ornaments, or that such a slender, flexible thing as a stalk should support a figure perched upon it, or that roots and stalks should produce now flowers and now half-length figures? (*The Ten Books on Architecture*, trans. M. H. Morgan, p. 211)

## HISTORICAL NOTES

The evidence for sophisticated cultures in the Aegean area takes us back to at least 2000 BCE; but it was around 800 BCE, after a "dark age" brought on by a wave of invasion, that the rise of what we consider classical Greece began. The Dorian Greeks who had invaded mainland Greece 400 years earlier had pushed the inhabitants of the mainland Mycenaean culture onto the Aegean Islands and the coast of Asia Minor. These peoples became known as Ionians. Over time, the distinct variations of a common architecture developed, but rarely does a group of people live in isolation; the seafaring Greeks were influenced by Egypt and other Middle Eastern cultures both in building methods and design and in decorative motifs.

The nomadic Dorians were reliant on deities of the sky and considered them as male forces, while the Ionians, whom they overran, had settled into the agricultural devotion to a mother earth goddess. The pragmatism of nomads supported a rational approach to architecture and the arts, while the agrarians were inclined to see the world in mysterious, emotional, and sensual terms. In both groups, myth was later supplanted to some extent by philosophies which encouraged a different sort of inquiry into the order of the natural world: "As nature and human nature were not

distinguished, that Order was seen as moral as well as material" (Christopher Tadgell, *A History of Architecture*, vol. ii, p. 31). The Pythagoreans and other philosopher-mathematicians believed that the soul's release was dependent on the knowledge of truth, which for them was the harmony of numbers, the ultimate good beyond the transient, subjective world of observation. These and similar ideas formed the basis of classical architecture, and discouraged deviation from the essential building type: the rectangular temple remained the same for several hundred years. It is interesting to compare such a static approach to the great variety of cathedrals erected in France—Reims, Amiens, Chartres, and Notre Dame de Paris—which were all designed and built in a relatively short period of time in the early to mid-thirteenth century. For the Greeks the emphasis was not on creating new species of architecture, but on refining and perfecting the existing ideal. And maybe it is this heroic seeking for the perfect harmony that has ensured the survival of classical architecture.

By 700–600 BCE there was a unifying Hellenic culture among the peoples of the Aegean area (though they were not united in government), and there is no doubt that wooden structures had been erected to house their deities. *Architekton* originally meant "master carpenter". The invention of clay roofing tiles in the eighth century BCE necessitated peaked roofs with a substantial supporting structure. The use of post-and-beam, or column-and-lintel, construction is known as the **trabeated** system of building. The transition to stone in place of timber was swift.

For two centuries builders experimented with the basic temple form, laying out ever larger rectangular floor plans and making columns more slender—pushing the envelope, as it were. With a studied confidence, this temple type was eventually transferred to other kinds of structures: meeting places (*stoas*, which were long colonnaded porticos), gates, and tombs. This flexibility may be another reason why ancient Greek architecture has endured. The widespread diffusion of Greek civilization, partly due to the conquests of Philip II of Macedonia and his son Alexander the Great (356–323 BCE), is also a factor in the survival of Greek architectural ideals.

Throughout subsequent history the Parthenon has been thought of as the quintessential classical structure. Built during the age of Pericles (444–429 BCE), it seems to incorporate all the accumulated subtleties of classical endeavor. There is a much better example of

*Fig 1.1 The Theseion or Hephaesteum, Athens (449–444 BCE), the best-preserved example of a Greek Doric temple, viewed from the southwest (by courtesy of the American School of Classical Studies at Athens: Agora Excavations)*

the Doric temple, however. The Theseion, built just prior to the Parthenon (449–444 BCE), is the most intact Doric temple today (Fig 1.1). It is also known as the Hephaesteum, as it is thought to have been dedicated to Athena and Hephaestus. Its architect used all the accumulated knowledge of optical refinement and proportion to make the structure look strong and vibrant, especially as viewed from the Agora (marketplace) nearby. It is massive and masculine, though not as heavily proportioned as earlier examples. It can be contrasted with the lighter and more decorated Erechtheion (421–405 BCE) (Figs 1.2 and 1.3) and temple of Athena Nike (427 BCE) (Fig 1.4), both of the Ionic order. These buildings represent the two original

*Fig 1.2 The Erechtheion, Athens (421–405 BCE). At center, the Ionic colonnade of the east front; at left, the famous caryatid porch, with carved figures in place of columns (by courtesy of the American School of Classical Studies at Athens)*

*Fig 1.3 A reconstruction of the east front of the Erechtheion, from Cyril M. Harris,* Illustrated Dictionary of Historic Architecture *(by courtesy of Dover Publications, Inc.)*

orders, as discussed more fully below. The third, the Corinthian order, developed as a variation of the Ionic, and the main difference is in the treatment of the capital. It reached its classical form somewhat later, in the first century BCE; the Greeks rarely used it, leaving its

widespread use to the Romans. (The Tower of the Winds in Athens, built in 334 BCE, seems to represent a transitional style; at least, the capital used there is a hybrid variety where acanthus leaves and stiff leaves are combined in a flared, bell-shaped form. For a

*Fig 1.4 The temple of Athena Nike, Athens (427 BCE), Ionic order (by courtesy of the American School of Classical Studies at Athens)*

pilaster version of this capital, see pages 119–22.) These are the three orders which the Romans, in their fascination with Greek culture, took as their own.

## THE ROMAN CONTRIBUTION

Roman architecture was not merely inspired by previous Greek efforts, but was dependent upon the basic tenets of Greek design. Yet the Romans introduced and/or developed three new engineering methods in which they surpassed the masters of stone temples. These were the stone arch, the roof truss, and the use of cement.

The arch, borrowed from the Etruscans, allowed for the development of vaults and domes, with all the structural and stylistic possibilities inherent in the form. In fact, a whole new system of structural principles, called the **arcuated** (as opposed to trabeated) system, came into play. The most spectacular examples are the multi-tiered arches of aqueducts or of the Colosseum in Rome.

The Greeks had used timber beams for roof rafters, but internal support columns were needed for large spans. Developing the triangulated roof truss allowed the Romans to span much broader spaces without interruption. Roman temples tend to be less narrow than their Greek antecedents for this reason.

Lastly, the Romans discovered or invented a natural cement in the early second century BCE. Though the process for making concrete had been known in previous periods and was used by the Greeks, it was the Roman discovery of a volcanic material (pozzuolana) which made the mix both cheaper and superior to previous recipes. This discovery revolutionized the technique, if not immediately the form, of building. Smaller stones and bricks were used in conjunction with the new material to build more complex forms. It seems that everything was built of brick and mortar: baths, gymnasiums, libraries, aqueducts, triumphal arches, as well as temples.

The Romans introduced two further orders of architecture: the Composite, which fused the Ionic with the Corinthian; and a simpler form, the Tuscan. Though mentioned by Vitruvius, the Tuscan order was little used until the Renaissance. The ultimate example of these innovations is the temple to the Pantheon of gods erected by Emperor Hadrian in 120 CE. It is a domed building measuring 142ft (42.3m) in diameter as well as in height.

It is to a Roman writer that we owe much of what is known of classical architecture apart from the ruins themselves—which, of course, archaeologists are still excavating. Marcus Vitruvius Pollio, writing in the first century BCE, produced *De architectura* (translated by M. H. Morgan as *The Ten Books on Architecture*), a treatise on building and architecture, covering everything from where to locate a city to slaking lime for cement, from the water organ and other machines to astrology and the acoustics of the theater. Among these curiosities are notes on symmetry and proportion, and the first systematic presentation of the orders of architecture to have survived. Republished repeatedly since the early sixteenth century, these observations and codifications have had an incalculable influence on all of Western architecture, being filtered through the

*Fig 1.5 The Villa Almerico at Vicenza, Italy, by Andrea Palladio, begun in 1566 (by courtesy of Carroll W. Westfall)*

*Fig 1.6 The Rotunda of the University of Virginia, Charlottesville (1817–26), designed by Thomas Jefferson and modeled after the second-century Roman Pantheon*

writings of later authorities such as Leon Battista Alberti (1404–72), who wrote the first major Renaissance work on (Roman) architecture, *De re aedificatoria,* in 1450; Andrea di Pietro della Gondola, better known as Palladio (1508–80), whose *Four Books of Architecture* made him perhaps the most influential figure in the preservation of classical ideals next to Vitruvius himself; and Giovanni Lorenzo Bernini (1598–1680), whose baroque interpretations are the most flamboyant incarnation of classical motifs.

Renaissance classicism was brought to England by Inigo Jones (1573–1652) after a trip to Italy in 1601. Through the influence of many British architects, such as Sir Christopher Wren (1632–1723), James Gibbs (1682–1754), and Robert Adam (1728–92), classicism came to America. As the colonists were dependent on the mother country for most manufactured goods, so too for the designs for building "in the latest style". Design or pattern books by Sir William Chambers (1723–96), Batty Langley (1696–1751), and Abraham Swan (*The British Architect*, 1745) were amongst those to be found in the libraries of the wealthy, whether in the rural South or the cities of the North. In America itself, Asher Benjamin (1773–1845) wrote several influential works, borrowing heavily from others. President Thomas Jefferson (1743–1826), in the tradition of the amateur architect, designed a number of residential buildings (including his own), as well as public ones including the University of Virginia and the Virginia State Capitol. Palladio's Villa Almerico or Villa Rotonda, begun in 1566 (Fig 1.5), is not so far from the

historical examples it emulates, and Jefferson in turn is not far behind in designing the University of Virginia Rotunda after the Pantheon in Rome (Fig 1.6).

## THE ELEMENTS OF CLASSICAL DESIGN

To be a competent architectural carver, one does not need to memorize all the minutiae of classical examples, but a carver should understand the underlying principles. Reading the various sources, one realizes that in spite of the reverence for the orders there is much variation in the Greek and Roman archetypes. Even Vitruvius' descriptions do not match some existing examples. Sir Banister Fletcher in his *History of Architecture on the Comparative Method* shows six different profiles of the Doric column capital and as many different Ionic columns, all taken from existing ruins. Evolution of style or construction may account for these variations, but nevertheless a generalized type is easily recognizable. Though I would emphasize the need for accuracy in reproducing the details of a particular order, one can extrapolate them to fit a particular need, as indeed designers throughout the centuries have done (Figs 1.7 and 1.8). For example, the Ionic capitals described in Chapter 6 have been adapted for columns used as communion table legs.

### PROPORTION

It is easier, especially when measurement standards vary, to transfer information for construction if there

*Fig 1.7 The front door of the Hammond–Harwood House, Annapolis, MD (by William Buckland, 1773–4) is typical of the eclectic use of classical motifs by later designers (by courtesy of the Hammond–Harwood House Association)*

*Fig 1.8 A detail of the same doorway, showing essentially an Ionic entablature with pulvinated frieze and dentils, but with modillion blocks of the Corinthian order added (by courtesy of the Hammond–Harwood House Association)*

are geometric methods to describe the process. The use of a triangle of 3, 4, and 5 units on each side to establish a right angle is a common example, familiar to carpenters even today. The systematic use of proportions was part of this methodology. Proportion as defined by Vitruvius is "a correspondence among the measures of the members of an entire work, and of the whole to a certain part selected as standard" (p. 72).

Strictly speaking, a proportion is an equality between two ratios—a ratio being a mathematically expressed relationship between two numbers (measures). For example, if one photograph measures 6 x 4in (a standard-sized print), the ratio between its sides is 6 : 4 or (dividing 6 by 4) 1.5. A blow-up of the photo measures 12 x 8in. Again, 12 ÷ 8 = 1.5. The photographs are in exact proportion, because their sides have the exact same ratio. Almost everyone is familiar with

the ratio of a circle's diameter to its circumference, known by the symbol $\pi$ (pi) and expressed approximately as 3.14; this ratio holds true for all circles.

Computer calculations to millions of decimal places notwithstanding, the Classical Age of architecture was one dominated by mathematics. Every part of the temple had a relationship to every other, the unit of measure being taken from the structure itself. Simple ratios based on the square and the circle were explored by Pythagoras and others. These basic shapes were regarded as "perfect" forms and imbued with mystical properties of eternity and divinity.

For example, the proportions of the Parthenon were minutely laid out with a predominant ratio of 4 : 9. The rectangle of the **stylobate** or floor is two and a quarter times longer than it is wide—a 4 : 9 relationship. The end elevation, excluding the stylobate and **pediment**,

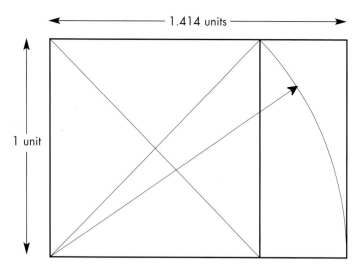

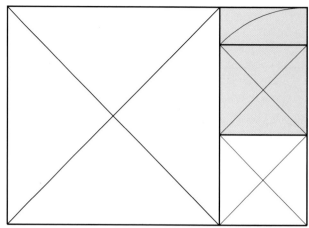

*Fig 1.9 The √2 rectangle: (a) constructing a rectangle of √2 proportion: the length of the rectangle is equal to the diagonal of the square from which it is derived*

is 4 units high by 9 units wide. The Theseion (see Fig 1.1) has similar proportions to the Parthenon. There are some subtle exceptions to this seeming rigidity. The corner columns of the façade are spaced more closely, so that the absence of background between them does not make them appear thin; the columns lean inward, and each has a slight outward bulge or **entasis**. These and other adjustments all serve to counteract visual imbalances.

Whole-number ratios, easily measured whatever the unit of measurement used, can be constructed easily with straightedge and compass. As early as Vitruvius, the characteristics of classical buildings were quantified in terms of a unit called the **module**. Vitruvius defines this as half the diameter of the column at its base, in the case of the Doric order, and as a whole diameter in the Ionic and Corinthian orders. To avoid the potential confusion here, this book uses the whole diameter as the unit of comparison. Because subdivisions of the module are needed to define smaller elements such as moldings or the parts of capitals, the module is divided into smaller parts. The half-column module is divided into 30 minutes and the full column into 60 minutes; thus the two methods turn out to be equal in practice. Notice in Figs 1.19 and 1.21 Palladio's use of minutes to subdivide each element of the **entablature**. The module of different Doric temples varies, and will be different again from an Ionic one. Every detail of classical architecture can be analyzed using this system of measurement.

There are a number of more complex proportional systems. Leaf through any of the Renaissance books on architecture, and it is obvious how important they are

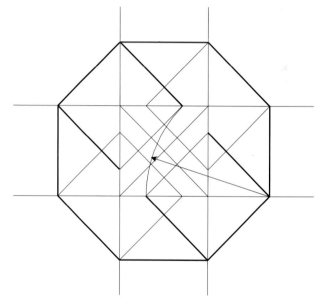

(b) *Constructing a regular octagon from overlapping √2 rectangles*

to the classical tradition—though, as Sebastiano Serlio (1475–1554) states, "from this proportion there can be no rule in number well set downe" (*Five Books of Architecture*, Bk. 1, Ch. 1, fo. 11). Two examples are the √2 (root-2) rectangle and the golden mean.

## The √2 rectangle

First articulated by Vitruvius, the √2 rectangle was widely used in the Renaissance. It is easy to draw this rectangle, because it makes use of a square and an arc (Fig 1.9). The reason this is termed a √2 rectangle is that the length of the long side derives from the square's diagonal. Since a square has right angles, its diagonal obeys the Pythagorean theorem: $A^2 + B^2 = C^2$. If the sides of the square are taken to be 1, then $C^2 = 1^2 + 1^2$, which is 2; therefore $C = \sqrt{2}$ (the square root of 2), which is an irrational number, or an endless decimal beginning 1.414. The rectangle which is added to the square in order to make a $\sqrt{2}$ rectangle, as shown on the right in Fig 1.9a, itself consists of a $\sqrt{2}$ rectangle added to a square. Cutting a $\sqrt{2}$ rectangle in half crossways creates two more $\sqrt{2}$ rectangles, and this useful property is exploited in the standard European "A" paper sizes. For example, the commonly used A4 paper, which is slightly larger than the format of this book, is made from a standard A-size sheet halved four times—cut it in half once more and you get A5, and so on. The measurement from side to side of a regular octagon is a $\sqrt{2}$ rectangle plus a square or, to state this another way, the octagon comprises a series of overlapping $\sqrt{2}$ rectangles (Fig 1.9b).

## The golden mean
Another proportion that has infiltrated much artistic design in the West is called the golden mean, golden rectangle, or golden section (Fig 1.10). Stated simply,

this is the division of a line or a rectangle such that the smaller part is to the larger as the larger part is to the whole. In the case of a line, there is only one point on line AC (Fig 1.10a) which creates this relationship. It can be expressed as "AB is to BC as BC is to AC" (AB : BC = BC : AC), a ratio which turns out to be an endless decimal beginning 1.61803. To actually find this point, B, on a given line, AC, construct a right-angled triangle, ACD, whose height measures half its base. Placing the fixed leg of the compass on D, strike an arc from A to intersect the hypotenuse at E. With the fixed leg on C, strike a second arc from E to the line AC. Where this arc intersects AC at point B, the line is divided in the ratio of 1 : 1.61803, the golden mean. Fig 1.10b shows a simple construction for a rectangle of these proportions. When a square is subtracted from the rectangle, the remaining rectangle has sides of the same ratio as the original rectangle (Fig. 1.10c).

How mankind decided that this proportion was pleasing is anyone's guess, but the notion has been with us since ancient times, having been used by Egyptians and Druids alike. It has collected much

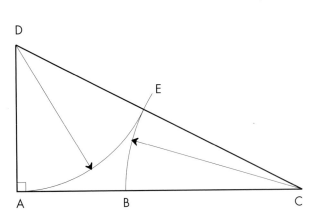

*Fig 1.10 The golden proportion:* (a) *dividing a line in the golden ratio (AB : BC = BC : AC)*

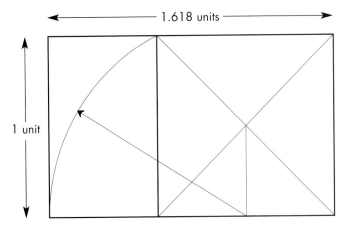

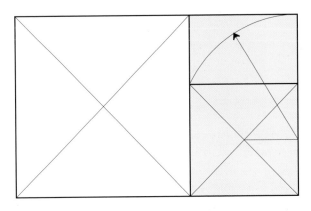

(b) *Constructing a golden rectangle*

(c) *Subtracting a square from the golden rectangle leaves another golden rectangle* mystical baggage along the way, but suffice it to say that the golden mean is an expression of man's interest and pleasure in proportion. (There are many other fascinating mathematical properties involved in geometry, such as the Fibonacci sequence, but these are on the fringes of our concern here.) Anything absolutely symmetrical is formal, authoritative, unyielding, pedantic. In some instances this is what is appropriate. To create a slight variance is more invigorating, inviting, and interesting. Obviously, too much variance and the design becomes out of balance, struggling, unsettling, and less than pleasing.

The notion of proportion as a pervasive aspect of design can be observed in most pieces of furniture as well as in architecture, because it is based on observation of the human figure (remember Leonardo's man spreadeagled within a circle and square?—it is straight from Vitruvius), and because much furniture design is derived from architectural models. Particularly outstanding in this regard are furnishings, picture frames, and interior details of the Renaissance, and those of the eighteenth century, when interest in the classical again flourished (Figs 1.11 and 1.12). (A good exploration of proportion as applied to an eighteenth-century tea table can be found in *Fine Woodworking*, #43.) Thomas Chippendale (1718–79), in his *Gentleman and Cabinet-Maker's Director* (1762), includes plates illustrating the orders, stating in the preface that "without an acquaintance with [the orders], and some knowledge of the rules of perspective, the cabinet-maker cannot make designs of his work intelligible".

## THE ORDERS

When we speak of the *orders*, we are referring to the entire configuration of the building, though in floor plan there is often no marked difference among them. Greek temples can be categorized into four general floor plans with variations, according to the placement

*Fig 1.11 This desk and bookcase made in Philadelphia between 1755 and 1765 is typical of the eighteenth-century revival of interest in classical ornament (collection of Mr and Mrs George M. Kaufman)*

*Fig 1.12 Detail of the Philadelphia desk and bookcase; the open pediment is a Renaissance variation on a classical feature (collection of Mr and Mrs George M. Kaufman)*

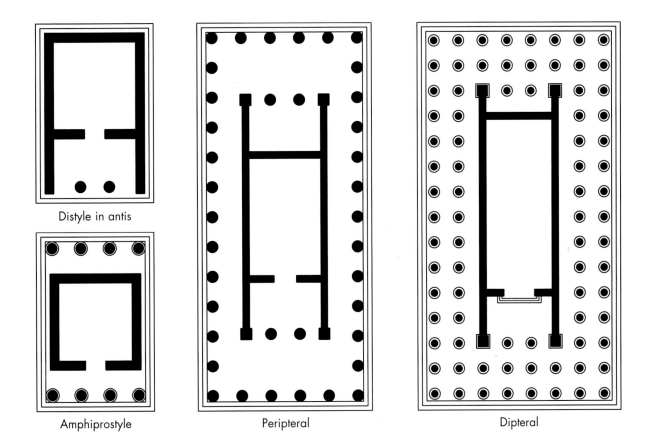

Distyle in antis

Amphiprostyle

Peripteral

Dipteral

*Fig 1.13 The four basic floor plans for classical Greek temples*

of columns around the main room or **naos.** In the first type the side walls (*anta*, singular and *antae*, plural) of the naos are extended and two columns are placed between them, which creates a porch, or *pronaos*. This is called a *distyle in antis* temple. This was probably the most numerous of the temple types. The second type places a row of columns front and back of the naos to create two porches, and is called an *amphiprostyle* temple. The temple of Athena Nike in Fig 1.4 is of this type. In the third, a row of columns, called a *peristyle*, runs along the sides as well as the ends. This type is called a *peripteral* temple. The Theseion of Fig 1.1 is of this type. The fourth type, in which a double row of columns surrounds the naos, is called a *dipteral* temple. Fig 1.13 illustrates these four different types. There are many terms to describe the number and spacing of the columns, which we need not introduce here.

All orders have their characteristic column and entablature (the entablature is the whole of the horizontal superstructure supported by the columns). The difference between the Doric and Ionic is seen clearly in the elevation: the proportions of the trabeated components—column width to height, and column height

to width of entablature—vary characteristically from one order to the other, as the illustrations on the next few pages will show.

Generally, the columns of Greek temples rest on a three-stepped foundation, the **crepidoma,** the top surface or "floor" of which is the **stylobate.** (One Roman innovation was to raise the temple floor on a much taller podium.) The Doric column does not have a base, though the Ionic and the Corinthian do, but all have distinctive capitals, and this is often the easiest way to identify the order. All varieties of column support a bearing plate, the **abacus,** which in turn supports the entablature or superstructure.

The entablature has three divisions. **Architrave** is the collective term for the beams spanning from one abacus to another. The **frieze** serves to cover the ends of the joists that rest on the architrave; in the Doric order, the **triglyphs** are said to represent the cross beams, the **metopes** the spaces between. The **cornice** projects over the lower two divisions and creates the eaves; it is made up of the projecting flat-faced **corona** and the surmounting **cymatium.** The latter usually has a **cyma recta** or **ovolo** molding profile (see Chapters 2 and 3).

*Fig 1.14 A fine Ionic portico at Jefferson's University of Virginia "grounds" (the local term for "campus"), showing a typical relief-carved pediment with acroteria*

At the peak and angles of the pediment are *acroteria* (**acroterion**, singular), which are decorative sculptures of **volute** and **palmette** (Fig 1.14; see also Fig 4.10) or, particularly in Roman structures, human figures (recall the Villa Almerico, Fig 1.5). Along the edges of the roof, covering the ends of the roof tiles, are *antefixa* (**antefix**, singular), again in the form of a stylized palmette (see Fig 4.9). Lions' heads with gaping jaws, spaced along the cymatium, act as waterspouts.

## Doric

The early Doric column was a squat one, 4.5–5 diameters high including the capital, while later versions were 6 or even 7 diameters high. The columns of the Theseion (see Fig 1.1) are 5.6 diameters in height. The Doric column is fluted, with sharp **arrises** between, and sits directly on the stylobate. The capital, shown with its various small details in Fig 1.15, consists of a bulging cushion shape, the **echinus**, supporting a square abacus. The width of the entablature is from 1⅓ to 2¼ diameters. The decorative features of the Doric order, apart from its geometric details, are the high-relief sculptures of the metopes, **tympanum**, and, in some cases, the pronaos (vestibule) frieze. Other orders also have high-relief sculpture, but it is the alternating triglyphs and metopes which are characteristic of the Doric order (see Figs 1.12, 1.15, 5.5, and 5.6).

The Roman adaptation of the Doric also has the metope–triglyph frieze, but the sculptures are static and stylized, usually of *bucrania* (bulls' heads or skulls; the singular is **bucranium**) or Apollo with sunbeams radiating from his head (Figs 1.16 and 1.17). Roman Doric also has rosettes around the column necking, as in Fig 1.16.

## Ionic

While the timber origins of the Doric order seem clear, the inspiration for the Ionic order is more conjectural; it was certainly influenced by Eastern motifs. The configurations of this order are more variable than the Doric, but generally present a lighter, more vertical appearance (Fig 1.18). The proportion of column diameter to height is approximately 1 : 9 (including capital), and the entablature is 2¼ modules or narrower. The column has a circular base composed of different profiles. The **Attic base** (so named by Vitruvius) is the most common, consisting of a **scotia** between two **tori**. The shaft is fluted, each flute being separated by a fillet. The capital (further discussed in Chapter 6) is distinguished by the double-scrolled element draped over an echinus molding.

The Ionic architrave has three subdivisions, called **fasciae**, which may be defined by an **astragal** but are otherwise undecorated. The uninterrupted frieze

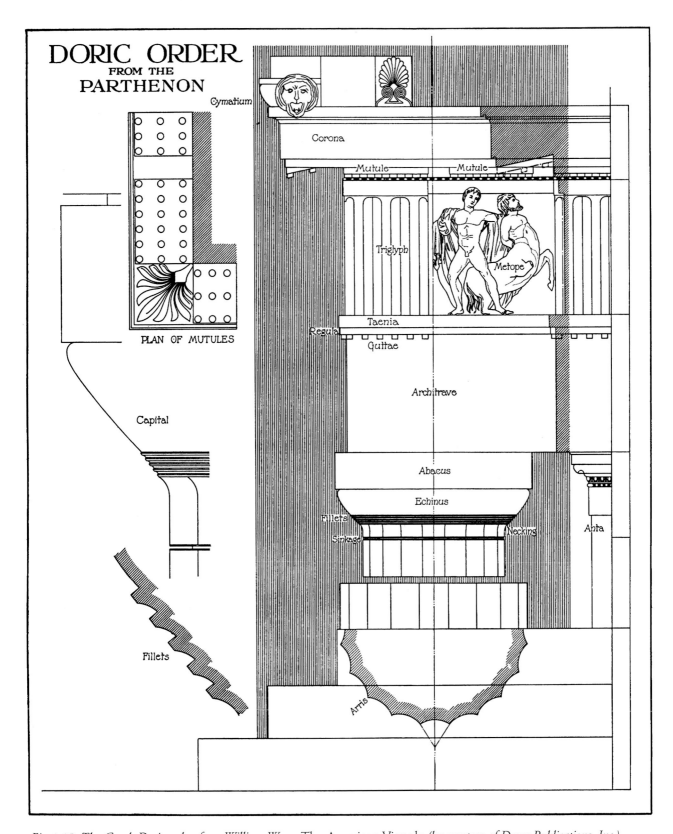

**DORIC ORDER**
FROM THE
**PARTHENON**

Cymatium

Corona

Mutule    Mutule

Triglyph

Metope

PLAN OF MUTULES

Taenia

Regula

Guttae

Capital

Architrave

Abacus

Echinus

Fillets

Necking

Sinkage

Anta

Fillets

Arris

Fig 1.15  The Greek Doric order, from William Ware, The American Vignola *(by courtesy of Dover Publications, Inc.)*

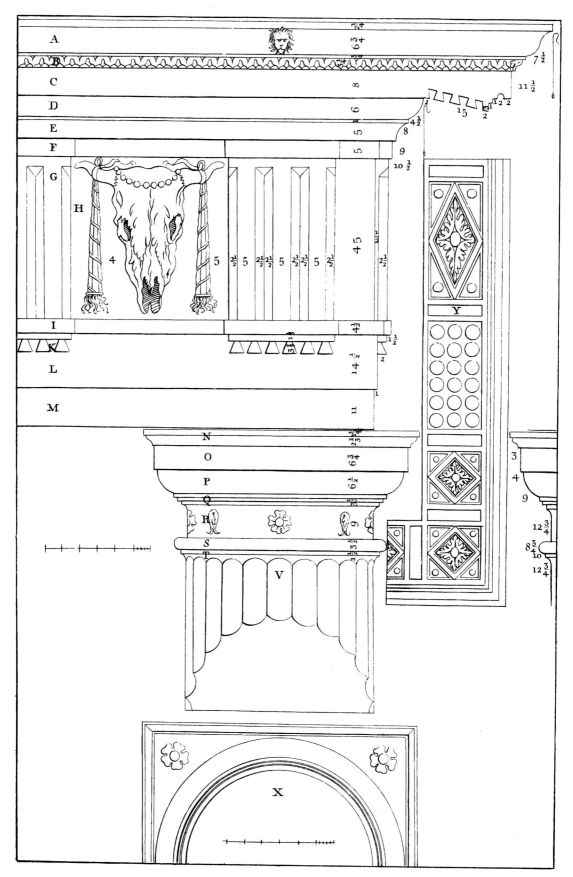

Fig 1.16  A decorated Roman version of the Doric order, including a bull's skull (bucranium), from Isaac Ware's 1738 edition of Andrea Palladio, The Four Books of Architecture (by courtesy of Dover Publications, Inc.)

*Fig 1.17 Doric frieze with head of Apollo in the metopes, on Pavilion I of the University of Virginia*

may be plain, or decorated with a continuous parade of sculptural figures. In later examples the frieze has a convex surface and is called a **pulvinated** frieze (Fig 1.19). The outstanding characteristic of the Ionic entablature is the **dentil** course, said to represent rafter or joist ends, which is placed between frieze and corona.

## Corinthian

The Corinthian order is proportionally similar to the Ionic, but tends to be even more slender, with proportions as much as 1 : 10 (Fig 1.20). Each element of this order is more ornate, and consequently it was used extensively by the Romans for its showiness. It does not derive organically from constructional necessity. The base can have a few more scotia and torus combinations, but the flutes of the shaft are the same as the Ionic. The capital is an inverted bell shape with acanthus leaves arranged in two rows, complete with tendrils that curl into volutes at the corners of the abacus; the abacus curves inwards at its sides, and projects at the corners. The entablature is similar to the Ionic, incorporating the dentil course, but somewhat taller. Its distinguishing feature is the **modillions** (scrolled brackets) projecting beneath the **soffit** or corona of the cornice (Fig 1.21).

## Composite

The Composite order is a later introduction, combining elements of the Corinthian capital with the volutes of the Ionic capital above it. For a rendition of the Composite capital, see Fig 6.86 on page 129.

## Tuscan

The Tuscan order is another late introduction by the Romans and is based on Etruscan antecedents. It is a simplified order, without decoration. Used on rustic structures and country houses, it serves as a kind of utilitarian order.

Each of the orders may also be embodied in the **pilaster**, which is a shallow rectangular version of the column, with similar base and capital, attached to a wall (Fig 1.22; see also Figs 1.11, 2.1, and 2.3).

Generally, Greek details, such as molding profiles, tend to be based on the ellipse or the parabola, and appear shallower and therefore "softer" than the Roman versions, which are based on the circle. (Fig 2.6 compares the two forms.) There is much evidence that the various elements were painted, whether carved or not, so the ruins which please us today as sculpture were much richer when originally built (see Fig 5.4). It must also be pointed out that the orders were sometimes mixed—the internal columns of the Doric Parthenon are Ionic, for instance—and so a hierarchy of placement developed, especially in Renaissance and Palladian designs. The Doric, being the sturdiest in appearance, tends to be used on the ground level, surmounted by the Ionic on the next level and finally the Corinthian on the upper stories.

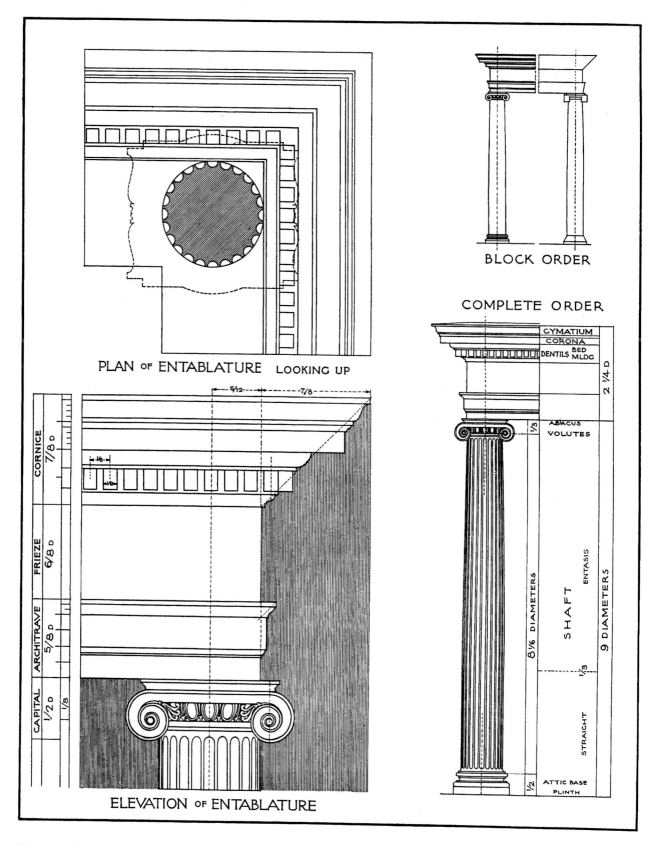

PLAN OF ENTABLATURE  LOOKING UP

BLOCK ORDER

COMPLETE ORDER

CYMATIUM
CORONA
DENTILS  BED MLDG
2 1/4 D

ABACUS
VOLUTES

CAPITAL 1/2 D
ARCHITRAVE 5/8 D
FRIEZE 6/8 D
CORNICE 7/8 D

5/12   7/8

ELEVATION OF ENTABLATURE

8 1/6 DIAMETERS

SHAFT

ENTASIS

9 DIAMETERS

STRAIGHT

ATTIC BASE
PLINTH

*Fig 1.18 The Ionic order, from W. Ware,* The American Vignola *(by courtesy of Dover Publications, Inc.)*

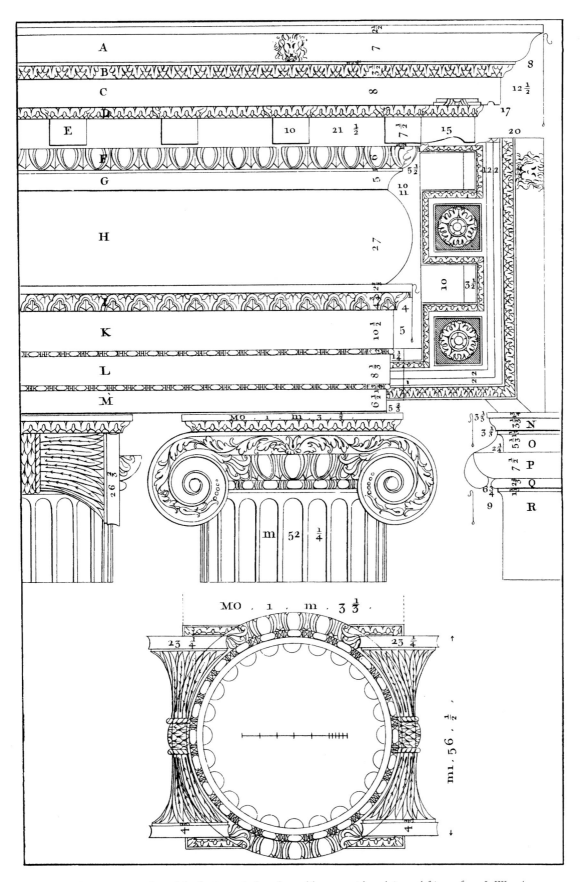

Fig 1.19 An ornate version of the Ionic capital and entablature, with pulvinated frieze, from I. Ware's Palladio (by courtesy of Dover Publications, Inc.)

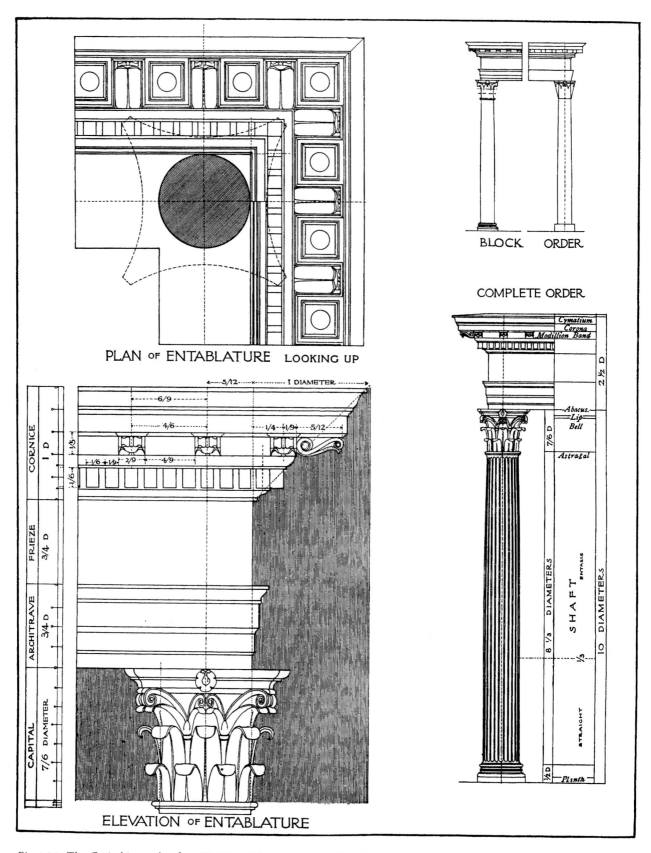

PLAN OF ENTABLATURE LOOKING UP

BLOCK ORDER

COMPLETE ORDER

ELEVATION OF ENTABLATURE

*Fig 1.20 The Corinthian order, from W. Ware,* The American Vignola *(by courtesy of Dover Publications, Inc.)*

Fig 1.21  A more elaborate Corinthian order, from I. Ware's Palladio; the acanthus-leaf modillions are marked E
in the side elevation, and are shown again in reflected plan on the right (by courtesy of Dover Publications, Inc.)

Fig 1.22 Corinthian column (left) and matching pilaster; all the traditional features of the orders may be adapted to pilasters as well as columns

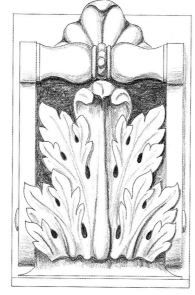

Fig 1.23 Front and side elevations of a voluted bracket (see Figs 7.36 and 7.37): an example of a three-dimensional rendering combining mechanical drawing and shading

## DESIGNING FOR CARVING

Designs are derived from the natural world or humankind's interpretation of it. Consequently, there are two broad areas of ornamentation: the naturalistic (however stylized) and the abstract, the geometrical. This dichotomy may seem simplistic, but the carver needs to blend the two skillfully into a pleasing composition. Composition is the overall integration or unity of the parts: each part is in a symbiotic relationship with every other part, essential and yet dependent. There are a number of properties which contribute to successful composition, such as symmetry, balance,

order, harmony, contrast, and so forth, all of which apply to art in general. In a three-dimensional medium such as woodcarving, however, there are further factors to consider. One must be concerned with the appropriateness of the design to the overall form: the decoration should not obscure the form or make the viewer perceive the underlying form as out of balance or proportion. The "structural" integrity of the piece must also be kept intact (remember Vitruvius' lament cited on page 2).

Abstraction or stylization must also be addressed. The less "meaning" an element has, the more it can be stylized, and consequently, the better it can bear repetition. The natural form is more often than not simplified and regularized by the carver—though the acanthus leaf, with its complex aesthetic evolution and stylistic diversity, is an important exception to this. The messiness of the real world is ignored, the more stylized the work becomes: a worm-eaten leaf is interesting and even desirable in a naturalistic carving, but out of place and confusing in a more abstract rendering. Decorative carving relies too much on repetition, unnatural placement, and distortion to accommodate randomly eaten leaves!

### DRAWING

It has been said that drawing is the basis of all good craftsmanship, and the importance of this activity in regard to woodcarving cannot be over-emphasized. Equally, one could say that mindful observation is the precursor to drawing; and this in turn derives from a sense of fascination, of wonder at the external world. Architectural ornament requires two different kinds of drawing: drafting and freehand drawing. For the architectural carver, one of the great attractions of the 1998 exhibition of Grinling Gibbons's work at the Victoria and Albert Museum was the numerous drawings in which Gibbons distinctively combines these two methods into renderings of proposed designs. The accompanying book, *Grinling Gibbons and the Art of Carving*, by David Esterly, reproduces many of these fascinating drawings.

Drafting, for the carver's purposes, usually involves basic procedures, a few simple theorems from Euclid and Pythagoras, and a sense of neatness. This sort of drawing is strictly practical: its aim is to represent several views of the object, to show measurements either full size or to scale, and to plan the integration of the object into the surrounding structural framework of a building. Usually several drawings or cartoons are required to understand a carved element fully. There may be a **plan,** which shows the object as viewed from above, such as the floor plan of a house showing placement of walls, windows, doors. The opposite is a **reflected plan**, which depicts the building or (more usually) object from below. The lower part of Fig 6.6 is such a view of the Ionic capital. There are, of course, many instances in which a plan view of an ornament is completely unnecessary, as it can be represented more clearly in other views. In most cases the **elevations** are the most important, because they show a frontal view of the object's vertical sides, which is the aspect most readily perceived by the viewer. There can be front, left, and right side elevations, though the sides may be simply mirror images. Rarely is the back of an ornament shown, as this side will be attached to the substructure of the building. The last type of drawing is the **section**, showing the various depths of the carving (the relief or **profile**). This drawing indicates the boldness with which the element is treated, and can help to determine the time involved in actually carving the element. The "cut" surface through the element is indicated on the drawing by shading or by diagonal lines, as in Fig 2.6.

As a word of caution for the carver who is following an architect's or designer's drawings, it is wise to check the supplied drawings for errors by adding up measurements, comparing different views, and making sure you understand the sections. It is not a bad idea to redraw the carved elements or make tracings of them, especially if the supplied drawings are not full-sized. It can be a shock to realize how large things become in a cramped shop, when they fit on a sheet of paper so nicely!

Freehand drawing requires an understanding and appreciation of form and light. Practice frequently, and accumulate a portfolio. You must understand the underlying principles of mass and form before surface decoration can be handled properly. "Ornament is always determined by its relationship to what it decorates and by what carries it" (Porphyrios, *Classical Architecture*, p. 60). If you need help, there are numerous private and community-college courses available to get you started.

It is often necessary to combine these two methods of drawing in order to reach a presentable rendering of what is to be accomplished, especially if someone else needs to be able to visualize the final product or is footing the bill. A poorly conceived idea will never be redeemed by the techniques used to produce it. A drawing produced with drafting equipment, inked and then shaded, will often serve the purpose. The precision of the drafting will give clear directions to the fabricator of the blank, and will show the actual dimensions; the shading allows the viewer to see the depth, the three-dimensionality of the proposed project. A black colored pencil that has a wax rather than graphite base is best, as it will not smear and will photocopy more readily (Fig 1.23). What is sought is a *representation* of what will be produced. The decorative design may sometimes be distorted in order to show it more fully, so that it would not, as drawn, fit the parameters of the mechanical drawing. A good example is the drawing of waterleaf designs in Fig 3.10 which, if drawn to conform literally to the cyma reversa profile, might inadvertently be made too short.

Some projects that involve multiple small elements, such as a vine or a branch with many leaves, can be composed by tracing only a few renderings of the element. First, the perimeter of the available space is drawn and, in the case of a vine, the flow of the central stem is sketched. Next, several of the leaves (or other elements) are drawn out to the appropriate size. Then a piece of tracing paper (which has also been marked with the outline of the area to be carved) is placed over the sketches and these are traced. The tracing paper is then shifted or turned over to be placed again over the initial sketches. By this method a string of leaves can be drawn quite quickly and, with some overlapping and variation, made to appear quite natural. Note that the leaves toward the end of the vine should diminish in size. This method is applied in Chapter 5 to develop a multi-layered rosette.

A logical extension of the two-dimensional visualization is modeling in a plastic material such as clay or Plasteline. A model in clay (a *maquette*) can clarify questions of depth and relationship that may be distorted or even undetected in a two-dimensional representation. It is not necessary to make a model of everything you desire to carve, but if you cannot easily visualize the finished product, or have trouble with human or animal faces or with anatomical relationships, then the time spent in modeling will increase your efficiency and pleasure in carving.

As a further aid, a practice piece can be carved from an extra blank or short piece of molding. It may be necessary to supply a sample to the client anyway, and a collection of samples is the best way of promoting your work. Further advice on layout will be given in suceeding chapters.

# CHAPTER 2

# MOLDINGS I

Working methods • Flat designs • Astragal • Ovolo • Frieze

The most common architectural decoration is the molding which, plain or fancy, is used for a variety of reasons: to create shadows, and therefore depth; to divide surfaces visually, creating balance or pleasing proportion; or to create a finished delineation to a corner, joint, or edge. There are functional uses as well: covering or weatherproofing joints, hanging pictures (as well as framing them), protecting plaster walls, and so forth. Moldings, for our purposes, are strips of wood (or edges of wider pieces) which have a distinctive shape or, more properly, **profile**; and it is this profiled part which is carved. Most of the plain profiles can be embellished with decoration; it is the repetition of design units which makes them effective

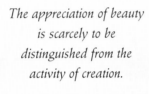

*The appreciation of beauty is scarcely to be distinguished from the activity of creation.*

H. E. HUNTLEY

in breaking up the inherent linear quality of moldings. Figs 2.1– 2.5 show some characteristic examples.

The plain profile can be fabricated or "run" by a computerized molding machine, stationary shaper, portable router, hand plane, or scratch stock. The architectural millwork firm specializing in custom work will use machinery to produce the profiles needed; they may use standard cutters or have someone on staff to grind the desired profiles. The shop without such equipment can use a combination of saws, handheld routers, and hand planes to fabricate the necessary shapes, particularly in the case of the smaller and more standard profiles. Large coves can be made on the table saw (see the discussion of picture

*Fig 2.1 Door architrave with Doric pilasters, full entablature, and open pediment, Gunston Hall (1759), Lorton, VA (by courtesy of the Colonial Williamsburg Foundation)*

Fig 2.2 A cornice at Jefferson's University of Virginia, Charlottesville (see Fig 1.6), showing (from top) modillion blocks and rosettes, egg and dart, and dentils

Fig 2.3 Detail of a mantel by the author (see Fig 7.24), showing Ionic pilaster with waterleaf abacus, and ovolo backband (photograph by Phillip Beaurline)

Fig 2.4 Scrolled pediment
on an overmantel at
Drayton Hall (1742),
Charleston, SC; the
moldings are egg and dart
and simple waterleaf (by
courtesy of Drayton Hall, a
National Trust Historic
Site/photograph Frederick
Wilbur)

Fig 2.5 A fragment from
the cornice of the
Erechtheion in the British
Museum, showing (from
top) leaf and dart, egg and
dart (each with bead and
reel beneath), and
anthemion (British
Museum/Frederick Wilbur)

frames on pages 138–40). Large rounds can be shaped with an ordinary bench plane. The small facets left from the plane can be smoothed by the use of a curved scraper, or with sandpaper; if the round is to be carved, many of the facets may be eliminated anyway. The table saw can be used to cut away excess material or to define the extent of a profile before molding plane or scratch stock is used.

There are many varieties of router bit available through numerous tool distributors, but their use may represent a compromise, especially when an existing profile is to be duplicated. It is possible to modify high-speed steel bits, but most molding bits are carbide-tipped and harder to alter.

Before the Industrial Revolution, moldings were made exclusively by hand plane and scratch stock. Each plane produced a specific profile, so the joiner required a chestful of them if he intended to undertake fine woodworking. There were planes for beads, coves, **ogee** profiles, ovolos, reeding, tongue-and-groove

*Fig 2.6 Drawing of molding profiles comparing Greek and Roman treatments, from Sir Banister Fletcher,* A History of Architecture on the Comparative Method *(by courtesy of the British Architectural Library, Royal Institute of British Architects, London)*

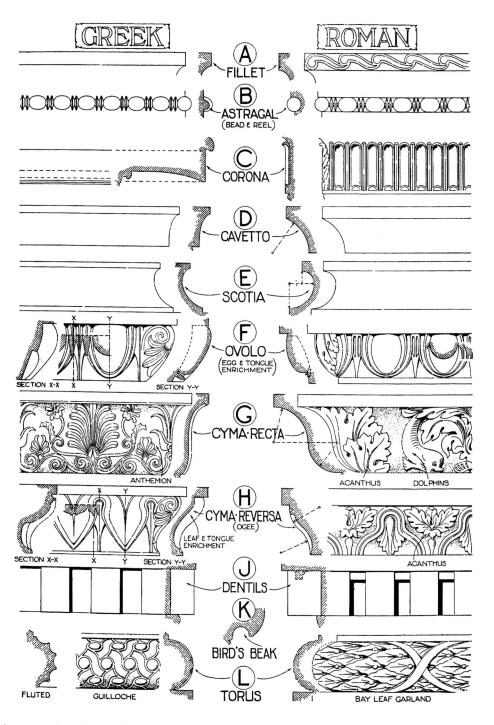

joints, and so forth. Some planes combined several profiles, such as cove, fillet, and ovolo, or bead and ovolo. The descriptive terms used by the practical joiner or carpenter for these profiles are not necessarily those used by the architectural historian: for example, round planes make cavettos, beading planes make astragals, while the common or Roman ogee, the Grecian ogee, and the reverse ogee planes all make different varieties of cyma profile.

There have been dozens of different profiles and combinations throughout history, but most classical ones can be assigned to a few families based on simple geometry (Fig 2.6). Most, in fact, are segments of a circle (or ellipse) or combinations of arcs in conjunction with flats or **fillets**. These families are: the half-round or **astragal** (more generically called the *bead*), with its big brother the **torus**; the convex quarter-round or quarter-ellipse, called the **ovolo**; the **cavetto** or *cove*, which is a concave quarter-circle or quarter-ellipse, with its sister the **scotia**, which contains two different arcs; and lastly the combination of two opposite arcs (one concave and one convex), the **cyma** or ogee. It must also be mentioned that many designs can be incised or cut into a narrow flat band: these include the **wave**, the **Greek key**, the **guilloche**, **chip-carved** designs, and many more.

This chapter discusses the astragal, the ovolo, and their cousins, as well as flat moldings.

# LAYOUT

The carver, then, is working on a seemingly tricky piece of material with curves and/or sharp edges in profile as well as a running pattern along its length. It will become obvious in this chapter that there is a correlation between the profile and the type of decoration which can be cut into it, and that the profile often dictates the tools used.

Moldings, by their very function, have to change directions around a room or piece of furniture, and the joint or corner is usually a miter, regardless of how the molding is applied. In quality work, whether door casing, mantel, or cornice, the most prominent elevation is laid out symmetrically. That is, the centerline falls between two of the main decorative units so they are equal in number on either side of the centerline; though at times a main unit is bisected by the centerline. Some designs—spiraled ribbons and **gadrooning**, for instance—have an orientation to right or left, so they originate from the centerline and proceed in opposite directions toward the ends or corners. So it is from the centerline that the basic increments of the pattern are laid out.

The point at which the miter cuts through the design determines whether adjustments are required in order to fit a whole unit in before the joint. Most patterns can be broken in two places: either at the midpoint of a design unit, so that the unit itself "turns" the corner, or between units. (Some moldings have several alternating units, affording a wider choice of break-points.) Many patterns can be "stretched" if necessary over several repeats so that the miter joint falls in one of these two places. Not all designs divide neatly at the miters, the egg and dart (an ovolo profile treated later in this chapter) being the primary example of one that does not—a half or a third of an egg meeting a half-dart would look ridiculous. The Greeks realized the awkwardness of this situation and either left the corner unornamented or "covered" the design with a leaf, one half of the leaf falling on either side of the joint. The latter solution has been adopted almost without exception ever since. The idea is that the concealing leaf tricks the eye into assuming that the underlying design is continuous, regardless of how the pattern actually would work out if the leaf were not there. Fig 2.7 shows a typical example, and others can be seen in Figs 1.21, 2.3, 2.55, and 2. 56, as well as Figs 7.6 and 7. 31.

Short lengths of molding, as in "dog-legs" on door casings or returns on cornices, if too short for a full unit, are sometimes treated with simplified or abbreviated renditions of the design (Fig 2.8). One molding which is not amenable to this treatment is the egg and dart.

*Fig 2.7 Egg and dart molding, showing the use of leaves to mask the miter joint*

Fig 2.8 *An example of the author's work, showing how an abbreviated version of a foliage design may be used for a short return section or "dog-leg" in a crossetted frame*

In order to have a nice-looking joint, the molding should be mitered and fitted dry before laying out the carving. The mitered pieces should be labeled in sequence so that the carving at the joints can be aligned accurately and appear as though carved *in situ*. Some

short pieces could actually be glued together prior to carving. Rarely would the situation arise that a molding is actually carved in place, however.

While laying out the design, remember that a flat drawing in elevation does not account for the actual curvature of the material; the design may need to be stretched in its apparent height to accommodate this three-dimensionality. This may, in turn, distort the proportions so much that the design along the length requires adjustments as well. One can easily see, for example, that the waterleaf designs in Fig 3.10*a, b,* and *c,* when actually carved, may appear narrower than depicted. Correction is made in the selection of the tools to be used. The sample is then carved. On the other hand, Fig 3.10*d* appears slightly stretched, but when carved it will have more depth and appear better proportioned.

You may have to redraw the repeating unit several times to make it look comfortable on the profile. After these necessary adjustments, use dividers to transfer the repeating unit to the remaining pieces of molding. Check measurements frequently, as a fractional variation tends to be cumulative and will "creep". Once a satisfactory layout has been achieved on one piece, it is prudent to lay out all pieces before work begins.

## THREE LAYOUT AIDS

### Marking frame

If there are multiple pieces of the same length, a simple marking frame can be made to mark increments simultaneously on all pieces (Fig 2.9). The lengths of molding should not be unmanageably long: door-panel molding is a good occasion to use this device. The

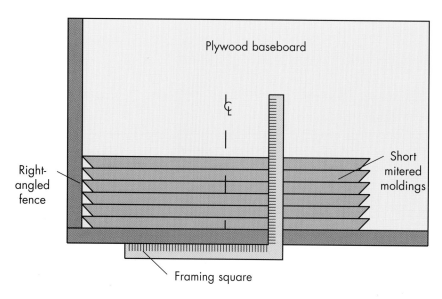

Plywood baseboard

Right-angled fence

Short mitered moldings

Framing square

Fig 2.9 *The marking frame: a simple jig for marking out moldings of uniform length*

frame consists of two strips of wood fastened to adjacent edges of a rectangular piece of plywood so as to form a right angle. If the profiled molding pieces are placed together against one fence and the ends pushed until they touch the adjacent fence, the centerlines on all pieces should match. A framing or try square can then be moved along the first fence to mark across all pieces at once.

## Marking wheel

Another aid to laying out unit increments is the marking wheel (Fig 2.10). This is simply a wheel with sharp points around its circumference, mounted in a handle. It is essentially a modification of the pounce wheel or scrivener's wheel used to space lines on parchment, or the seamstress's marking wheel. (These obviously have a limited range, even if modified by removing some of the teeth.) This gadget works best on smaller moldings such as bead and billet, waterleaf, and small egg and dart. Determine the required increments by carving a sample piece. The measurements between design units or half-units will determine the circumference of the wheel or disk. It is easy to divide the disk accurately into eight parts using 45° divisions, especially if the stock is dressed square to begin with. For example, if the increment desired is ⅝in (16mm) between leaves, beads, etc., multiply by 8 to obtain the required circumference, which in this case is 5in (128mm). (This example worked out nicely in imperial measurements!) Then divide this number by π (pi—approximately 3.14) to find the diameter necessary (remember: $C = \pi d$, where C is the circumference and d the diameter). Half this diameter gives the radius needed to draw the circle on the disk.

Choose the bolt which will be used as the axle of the marking wheel, and drill a hole the same size through the center point of the disk blank. Cut out the circle with a bandsaw or coping saw, allowing plenty of room on the outside. Put the bolt through the hole and use a nut to tighten the disk to the bolt. The bolt is then mounted in a Jacobs chuck on the lathe, and the disk is turned down until the circumference line is just shaved off. With a flexible plastic ruler or seamstress's cloth measuring tape, check to see that the divisions are equal and accurate. The disk should then be turned about ½₂in (about 1mm) smaller, to allow for the length of the points which are inserted next.

With a try square, carry the division lines onto the edge of the disk. Use a sharply pointed awl to mark each division in the middle of the edge. Hammer brads

*Fig 2.10  The marking wheel in use*

into these points, as straight in line with the division marks as possible, and with a wire cutter snip the nails off close to the disk. The raised peak created by the snippers is usually enough to mark the wood, but if preferred the points can be filed. In fact, a little adjustment can be made if necessary by filing the brad on one side only. Note that if the brads project too far the intended increment will be increased.

The handle is then made from ¾in (19mm) square stock and turned on the lathe. Leave a sufficient length of square at one end for cutting a slot on the table saw to house the disk. On the table saw, cut a slot somewhat longer than the disk radius, to accommodate different-sized disks. Drill a hole near the end of the slot with the same bit that was used to drill the disk. Rub a little paraffin wax on the wheel and mount it in the handle, then test it on a scrap piece of wood. If half of the original increment is required (⁵⁄₁₆in or 8mm in our case), run the wheel down the molding in the usual way and then begin again, setting one point halfway between the previous marks.

## Gauge block

One additional tool often useful in marking lines along the run of a molding is the gauge block (Fig 2.11). It is advantageous to have such lines when you need to locate a similar feature on each unit; a good example is the "eyes" of acanthus leaves. The gauge is a flat piece of stock of ½in (13mm) or so thickness, with a fence attached at 90° to it. (Most moldings have a 90° back or fillet which the gauge block can run against.) In the face of the stock drill holes of suitable size to hold

*Fig 2.11 The gauge block in use. The multiple holes allow more than one pencil to be used at a time if necessary*

hexagonal lead pencils snugly. The critical point is to locate these holes where they will mark the desired features. They should be measured directly from the molding which has been partially laid out or, better still, from the carved sample. With the fence against the back of the molding and the top face riding the molding, push the pencils through the appropriate holes until they touch the molding. Using the fence to guide the gauge, you can then move the pencils the length of the molding.

An old marking gauge with a hole drilled in it for a pencil can also be used, but the advantage of the gauge described above is that several pencils can be used to mark several lines simultaneously; it can also be used in tight situations where the arm of the marking gauge might be in the way.

Related trades may have various tools or aids which can be adapted to woodworking. The popularity of quilt-making has spawned a number of them, particularly plastic layout grids and squares.

## CREATING PATTERNS FOR LAYOUT

Some designs, such as bead and billet or egg and dart, are simple enough to warrant only the barest laying out. More complex designs, such as acanthus leaves, will require a more sophisticated layout and a pattern (see below, Figs 2.57 and 2.58). Because a concave or convex surface is to be marked, the material chosen for the pattern needs to be flexible, but able to retain the integrity of the profile. For sustained use, a thin metal

such as aluminum roof flashing or sheet brass will serve well. Making the metal stencil can be time-consuming and tricky at best, but the time saved in layout will offset any frustration in making a good stencil. One long side of the metal should be referenced to one edge of the profile by butting it up against a flat on the profile itself (Fig 2.12) or on the bench top. A 90° flange formed on one edge of the pattern can also serve to reference it against the edge of the profile.

For larger profiles without an obstructing fillet, sheet rubber of sufficient hardness and thickness (gasket rubber) can be used. A board which has a saw kerf along its length serves as a base. The molding to be marked is fixed to the board with its face at the edge of the groove. The rubber stencil is moved along this groove and pressed onto the profile. The groove prevents the rubber from shifting.

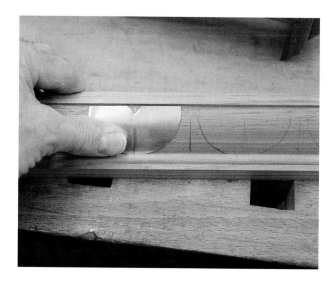

*Fig 2.12 Setting out egg and dart with the aid of a metal pattern. The pattern butts against the fillet at the top of the molding and the astragal at the bottom; the central notch is aligned with the penciled increment lines*

### Making a metal template

Transfer the design to the metal, or tape a paper pattern to the metal. There are two methods of actually cutting the stencil: the metal blank can be kept flat on a scrap board for cutting and then bent afterwards to conform to the profile, or it can be bent on a scrap piece of molding and retained there for cutting. In either case, the actual tools to be used in carving the molding are used to make the pattern. Take time to visualize how the stencil will be used: are you marking the areas to be left or those to be carved away? Do you need to leave connectors between cutouts? Make sure the metal is referenced correctly, and proceed to match the curvature of the gouges to the basic elements of the pattern, cutting through with a tap of the mallet. You will need to resharpen the tools, but if the volume of molding is sufficient, the time spent is well worth it. In making any stencil, the intention is to lay out the main cuts quickly, not necessarily marking every detail, but keeping the work crisp and tidy. A pencil is then used to transfer the pattern to the molding at each pre-measured unit. Check the layout carefully, as from here on the carving is done by eye.

# CARVING MOLDINGS

Because moldings are repeating and symmetrical patterns, the carver can produce large quantities efficiently. The usual method is to work the entire length with the same cut, then reverse the cut and work back to the beginning. The cure for the inherent boredom of such a procedure is to acquire a rhythm, and with it some degree of accuracy.

One aid to achieving this desired efficiency is to practice first on an extra length of the profile, so that the selection of tools and the sequence of cuts can be determined beforehand. Most moldings are in shallow relief, and the technique of "stab and relieve" is the general rule, keeping surface modeling to a minimum; in a sense, the profile of the molding itself provides the surface modeling. When replicating an existing design, the sweep of the tool must be matched to the shape of the design. Producing moldings is not so much a question of *accuracy* as *consistency*. Accuracy begins with layout and selection of tools, while consistency begins with experience in execution. Practically speaking, variations will occur and, unless these are grossly asymmetrical, the eye will be hard-pressed to detect them once the molding is installed. This, of course, is the more true the further the molding is from the viewer.

When working hardwood moldings, a mallet may be needed to set in. This should not be too heavy, as too much of a strike would "pop out" delicate pieces. Putting down and picking up the mallet for every placement of the tool is inefficient. This problem can be solved by turning your own mallet on the lathe, giving it a thin handle so that it can be held while the same hand is moving the gouge to the next repeat. A tough hardwood such as beech or dogwood works well. The mallet head only need be 2⅛–2¼in (54–57mm) in diameter, with a handle of ⅞in (22mm) diam-

eter at its narrowest. The overall length is 9¼in (235mm). Depending upon the wood, it will weigh 8–10oz (230–280g); the weight is not as important as the length of handle (Fig 2.13).

## HOLDING THE PROFILED MATERIAL

As with all work to be carved, the molding needs to be held solidly on the bench, and although the usual metal bench dogs or clamps serve well for most projects, we must be careful not to dub the sharp long points of mitered pieces. There are several ways to hold mitered profiles: wooden bench dogs can be modified, or special jigs made.

Using scrap hardwood, make two bench dogs with wider than usual heads (Fig 2.14). They do not need to have spring tensioners, but should fit snugly into the dog holes in the bench. Their protruding "chins" rest on the bench top. In the middle of the face of each dog, place a small screw, leaving ¼in (6mm) of the shank exposed. Remove the screw heads with a hacksaw and then grind or file the shanks to points. With a chisel,

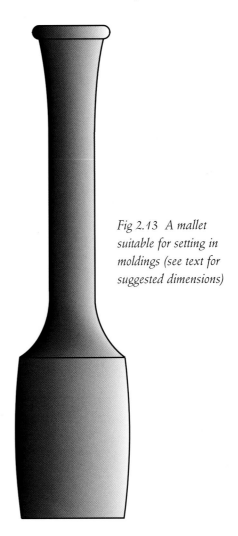

*Fig 2.13 A mallet suitable for setting in moldings (see text for suggested dimensions)*

Fig 2.14 Bench dogs for holding pieces with mitered ends

carefully pare the corners of the face backward from the screw so that the cheeks form an acute angle. With the dogs placed in the appropriate holes, the vise is then closed so that the points grab the mitered ends of the molding; the resulting marks will be hidden when the miter is assembled. This method works well for medium-sized moldings. The drawback is that only one length of molding can be done at a time (or two, on a bench with a double row of dog holes).

When a number of pieces of the same length are to be carved (as with molding for door panels), a jig can be made to hold the mitered pieces. A length of hardwood is used as a supporting fence upon which cleats are mounted to hold the ends of the molding. Depending upon the length of the molding and the

available area of bench top, several lengths may be mounted on one jig (Fig 2.15). The ends of the short cleats are cut at 45°. Drill screw holes in the cleats, then mount one of them to the end of the fence. Place a pre-mitered piece of molding snugly into the 45° space. Locate a second cleat at the other end, overlapping the mitered end slightly so that it holds it tightly. This second cleat can be made double-ended (as in the photograph) to accept a second piece of molding in line with the first. This fence or jig is then clamped to the bench top. The cleats can be remounted for different lengths of molding.

Another method is to screw through a waste board and into the back of the molding, then clamp the waste board to the bench. This works well for small moldings and those which are carved right to the edge, such as spiral designs on astragals. The waste board protects the bench top from errant gouge marks.

It is not very practical to glue long lengths of molding to a backing board. This often recommended method should be avoided, since it adds time to the job in clean-up, and with fragile carvings there is always the danger of breaking pieces when trying to extricate the carving from the paper. Most architectural pieces can be held by vise, clamp, or screw, or wedged in routed recesses or between fences. Never nail a molding directly to the bench top, as the molding might split in its securing or removing, to say nothing of scarring the bench top for life.

## DESIGNS FOR FLAT SURFACES

There are many embellishments that can be achieved with a minimum number of tools, and which do not require a molded profile to be effective. They are carved directly into a flat surface and, though not moldings by definition, they may serve the same purpose. They are used for narrow pieces sandwiched in among other moldings, and are not to be confused with the frieze, which will be discussed below (pages 50–1). They can consist of isolated designs or of a continuous repeat. Evenly spaced flutes, zigzag designs, incised lines, overlapping circles resembling coins or scales, are all examples of this technique (Figs 2.16 and 2.17). The simplest such decorations are **chip-carved** designs. The term "simple" is not meant pejoratively, though we tend to think of these as vernacular motifs; accuracy in layout is essential just because these shapes *are* simple.

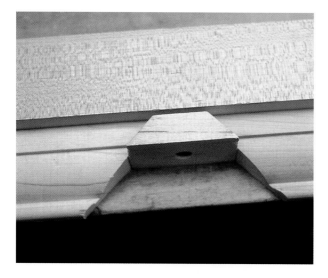

Fig 2.15 The jig for holding multiple pieces with mitered ends

Fig 2.16 *Setting in simple surface decoration; the fishtail chisel is angled to produce cuts which slope back from the surface*

Fig 2.17 *Subsequent stages in carving the same design. The result is very like traditional chip carving*

## THE FLUTE

Flutes can be carved using a single gouge, which is first stabbed straight in to make a stop-cut and then used to form the groove or flute which meets it. However, the acute corners created by this method are sometimes hard to clean out. For this reason the stopped flutes shown in Fig 2.18 tend to be preferred (see also Fig 3.2), but these require two tools: a firmer chisel modified to a round point, and a semicircular gouge. Flutes are commonly used on the cove moldings of picture frames (see Fig 7.20), mantels, and architraves, and can be grouped between rosettes to create the triglyphs of an ersatz Doric frieze (see Figs 7.45 and 7.46). These sorts of designs are found on vernacular furniture and

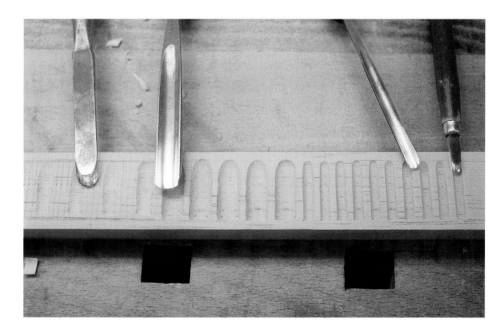

Fig 2.18 *Two sizes of flutes in a flat surface, with the tools used to cut them: a round-ended chisel and a semicircular gouge*

buildings everywhere, but often these techniques are incorporated into more complex elements, and it should be obvious that the few examples cited here only hint at the possibilities.

## THE FRET

The fret employs a slightly different technique, in that a definite ground is formed below the surface of the board, with the design remaining on the original surface. The fret is a geometric design based on the square or rectangle, and is also known as the **Greek key** or *labyrinthian fret*. The fret is perceived as a two-dimensional pattern, and lacks the interlaced effect of the guilloche, with which it is often confused. Fig 2.19 shows a simple Greek key design. The term *fret* is sometimes extended to include the use of segments of

*Fig 2.19  A simple Greek key fret*

circles, but these again are flat and two-dimensional, as the fret on a portico architrave in Fig 2.20 shows. In later periods, and particularly on furniture, the fret was made separately by drill and saw and then placed into a prepared recess, creating, in effect, the same appearance as that which is carved **in the solid**. Today, lengths of laser-cut fret ranging from Greek key to "Chinese Chippendale" can be bought and applied.

To lay out the fret, the gauge block or marking gauge is used to run parallel lines along the length of the piece, then the perpendicular lines are laid out with the aid of dividers. Mark the areas to be excavated; otherwise the numerous lines become confusing. Regularity is important. The lines can be stabbed in with a chisel and the ground excavated with a narrow frontbent chisel or shallow gouge.

## THE GUILLOCHE

The guilloche design is a series of circular bands or rings; it differs from the fret in that it uses two or more strands to form interlaced circles or **vesica piscis** shapes, with a definite implication of depth. Figs 2.21 and 2.22 show a simple rendition, while 2.23 shows two different-sized circles interlaced. In some cases the distinction between fret and guilloche may not be clear-cut—Fig 2.24, for example, is essentially a flat pattern, but slight relieving of the surface suggests interlacing strands—and a few coats of paint would obscure the distinction even further. The guilloche can

*Fig 2.20  Fret resembling a guilloche design on an architrave of the Semple house, Williamsburg, VA*

Fig 2.21 *Simple carved guilloche, showing both the basic structure and a typical style of ornamentation with rosettes and foliage*

Fig 2.22 *A similar guilloche on a Tudor cabinet*

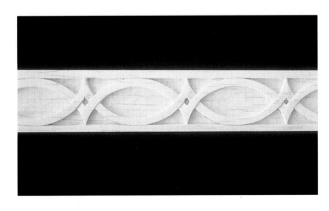

Fig 2.24 *An interlaced fret for a chair rail*

Fig 2.23 *Detail of overmantel with applied guilloche, Drayton Hall, Charleston, SC (Drayton Hall, a National Trust Historic Site/Frederick Wilbur)*

also be adapted to the astragal and torus moldings, where multiple rows of guilloche can look almost like macramé (see Fig 2.6, bottom left). Occasionally it can be found on shallow coves. Some Renaissance renditions combine squares and rectangles with circles, and are infilled with various flowers, shells, or other objects. The intertwining ribbons found sometimes on astragal moldings are a variety of guilloche.

To draw the common form is simply to construct overlapping rings (Fig 2.25a). For a given width of design, find the centerline and draw a circle the full width available. Decide how broad the rings will be, and overlap the next circle by that amount. Then, by measurement, the two series of circles (inner and outer) can be drawn. In carving the design, one strand is relieved so that it appears to pass behind the other; mark this clearly before carving begins.

With all designs of this kind, the tool curvature must precisely match the desired outline, especially when setting in vertically. This is necessary to maintain the flow of the line. In most of these shallow, essentially two-dimensional designs a perpendicular stab with the tool is possible. The flat ground is then cleaned with a shallow gouge. Because of the nature of these designs there are many deep recesses, for which the use of frontbent tools is almost mandatory. Repeated setting-in and relieving in this fashion will achieve the desired depth. Avoid a prying motion with the frontbent tool, using it only to clean out what has previously been set in.

It may be desirable to elongate the circle into a vesica piscis, either to accommodate flowers or to wind around an astragal; offsetting the center point of the arc to either side of the centerline will achieve this. Fig 2.25b shows an example. As when drawing circles, the width of the overall space available for carving is divided by a centerline. The center of the arc, however (labeled A in the figure), is placed off this centerline. The arc BC is drawn, the width of the strand decided, and a second arc drawn from D to E. The measurement between C and E determines the overlap of succeeding units. The opposing arcs are then drawn (with center F) to complete the vesica piscis shape. After establishing the centers, draw secondary lines parallel to the primary centerline; additional units can then be drawn efficiently using these secondary lines. The small increments are easily determined by using the same settings of the compass as were used for the original construction. There should be a diamond or lozenge shape where the two bands overlap. Experimentation will reveal a number of possibilities; Fig 2.25c and d show how the proportions change depending on whether the centers of the arcs are offset by a smaller or larger amount from the centerline of the design.

*Fig 2.25 Drawing the guilloche*

*(a) simple form constructed from overlapping circles*

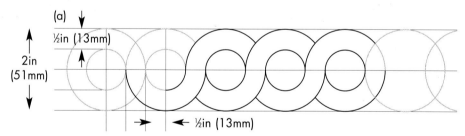

*(b) elongated or vesica piscis form, constructed from intersecting arcs*

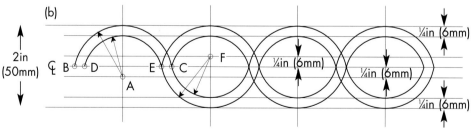

*(c) and (d) changing the proportions by varying the distance between the centers of the arcs and the centerline of the design*

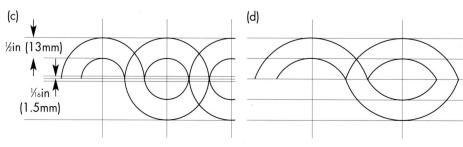

Fig 2.26 Wave design at base of eighteenth-century cabinet (Colonial Williamsburg Foundation/Frederick Wilbur)

## THE WAVE

Another classical design which is often found on flat bands is the **wave** or running scroll, a common motif in antiquity (Figs 2.26–2.29). It is carved in the same way as the guilloche.

Conceived in terms of a single line, the wave design is a series of regularly reversing spirals. When one (the upper) side of this line is recessed, the wavelike appearance is accentuated. The line spirals in toward a point of radical reversal, then "unwinds" to a second point of reversal, more gentle than the first, in order to repeat the inward spiral.

After several repeats have been established, the design is transferred to the material and set in as for a fret or guilloche. The motif is usually fairly small, so the volute can be sketched satisfactorily by eye. In fancier renditions, foliage sprouts from the volutes or flies like foam off the crest.

Fig 2.28 Symmetrical waves with central bead

Fig 2.29 Wave with floral ornament, probably in plaster, on a stairway in the British Museum (British Museum/Frederick Wilbur)

Fig 2.27 The wave design at its simplest

# THE ASTRAGAL MOLDING

**Bead** is a general descriptive term referring to any profile which is half or more of a circle in section, and comparatively small in relation to surrounding moldings (Fig 2.30). The **cock bead** is a small half-round raised from the surrounding surface, and is often used on furniture to emphasize shapes or define edges, particularly around drawer fronts. The **quirked bead** lies flush with the surface of a board but is separated from it by a valley (the quirk) on one or both sides. The *corner bead* (or *return bead*) runs along the edge of a board and has quirks on both sides. The **astragal** is the half-round molding flanked on one or both sides by a flat ground, or fillet (though **fillet** more properly refers to a projecting flat). The term *astragal* is more often used when the bead molding is ornamented with carving.

The bead is commonly found on many decorated items, from silverware to cast-iron lampposts, and on many styles and types of furniture. It is found as an edging or inner molding on picture frames, as an inner molding on door casings (where a square corner would tend to be worn away or cause injury), and in conjunction with other moldings in the **backbands** of fireplace surrounds. It is the lower molding (just under the egg and dart) of the echinus on an Ionic capital. Many of the illustrations in this book show the relationship of the astragal to other moldings. In fact, in almost any instance where there are several tiers of moldings the bead is tucked in somewhere, in which case it plays a secondary role to the larger, more decorated moldings.

The astragal can be carved in a variety of ways. The most common shapes are hemispherical domes (confusingly referred to as *beads*), sometimes combined with oblong billets (*bead and billet*, also known as *berry and sausage* or *bead and spindle*) or with concave or vesica piscis shapes (a kind of "squashed" bead) which

are called *reels*, thus **bead and reel** molding (see Figs 2.5 and 2.38). The diameter of the half-round, of course, can be as small as ⅛in (3mm) or as large as several inches. Much larger than this, and the profile becomes a **torus** molding. The torus is found in the bases of columns, and occasionally running around the base of a structure. On column bases it is found in conjunction with the **scotia** (see Fig 1.21, showing Palladio's Corinthian order, and Fig 2.6).

It is hard to do much with a bead molding as small as ⅛in, except for the familiar bead and billet molding. Any number of beads can separate the billets, but two, three, or five are usual. Billets are generally singular, and as long or longer than the cluster of beads that separates them. Larger-diameter astragals allow for further decoration, including spiral designs such as ribbon and flowers, overlapping leaves, and guilloche designs.

## CARVING THE ASTRAGAL

Carving beads is straightforward and two or three tools will accomplish the job. In order to obtain a hemispherical bead, the divisions along the molding need to be the same as the diameter or width of the molding (or slightly larger to allow for working room). In historical examples, beads are sometimes separated with flat ground between them and sometimes linked with a small rod. Ideally, however, the beads should just touch one another like a string of pearls (Figs 2.31 and 2.32).

Use the layout wheel to mark these divisions. Small pieces can be held by jamming them into a grooved board as seen in Fig 2.33. Begin by making stop-cuts between the elements with a carver's chisel, held at right angles to the run of the molding, using a light tap of the mallet. This step is necessary so that the tops of the beads don't pop off in subsequent operations—retrieving little hemispheres and gluing them back in place is inefficient, to say the least.

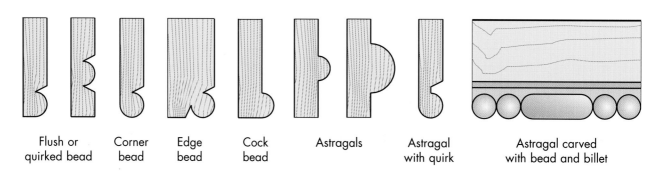

| Flush or quirked bead | Corner bead | Edge bead | Cock bead | Astragals | Astragal with quirk | Astragal carved with bead and billet |

*Fig 2.30 Molding profiles: the bead or astragal family*

*Fig 2.31 Fragment with ribbon and flower, and beaded astragal, Lenygon Collection (Colonial Williamsburg Foundation/ Frederick Wilbur)*

*Fig 2.32 Beaded picture frame (collection of Thomas Goddard)*

*Fig 2.33 Carving sequence: beginning the bead with tool low to the molding, concave side of blade facing downward*

*Fig 2.34 Finishing one side of the bead, with the gouge raised to perpendicular*

Next, a semicircular #9 gouge must be chosen to match the diameter of the bead. It is turned over so that the gouge sweep echoes the shape of the molding, and held in line with the run of the molding (Fig 2.33). The #9 is a deep gouge whose sharp wings will dig into the background if not handled carefully; grinding the wings back slightly prevents them from digging into the ground.

Beginning at the midpoint of each division with the tool parallel to the molding, raise the handle of the tool at the same time as applying cutting pressure to its forward motion. On softwoods the gouge can be raised to the vertical position as in Fig 2.34 and the half-bead formed in one motion, but when working hardwoods

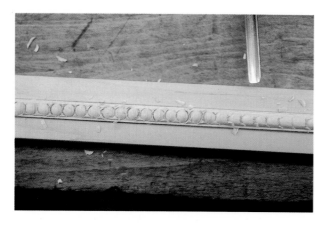

*Fig 2.35 Appearance of the molding after the first procedure: beads are fully formed but ground remains to be cleared*

*Fig 2.36 Using a #7 gouge to define the circular outline of the bead*

*Fig 2.37 The beaded astragal complete*

it is nearly impossible to do this. In the latter case, forcing the blade down will split off the top of the next division, because of the wedging action of the blade thickness. The safest method is to work in stages, taking a little off one side of each bead, then going back to do the same on the other side. Several passes up and back should have the beads down to the background (Fig 2.35). It is better to have a light touch and have to cut again than to be too dashing and end up with little Mount Fujis. Your technique will also depend on the size of the molding.

There may be triangular pieces still clinging between the beads; a skew or a fishtail chisel can be used to lift these pieces out. This may be difficult when the bead is nestled into the face of a board, separated only by a quirk, or next to a bolder shape such as an ovolo (as in egg and dart molding); in this case, an appropriately sized #7 gouge can be used vertically to cut the triangular piece from between the beads (Figs 2.36 and 2.37).

The bead and billet ornament is made by exactly the same technique: the billet is simply a length of plain astragal with a half-bead formed at each end.

## Variations on the bead

Bead and reel is a common variation (Fig 2.38). The reel is the opposite of the bead in that its ends are concave. The girth of the reel is oriented perpendicular to the length of the molding, just like the bead; a short section of the original half-round profile is usually left between the two concave ends. It is easier to carve all units as beads and then return to those designated as reels, though on many examples the reels are more narrowly spaced than the beads. Using a #7 gouge, slice across the grain from the top, working both sides down to the ground. The common Greek bead and reel consists of a single bead with two narrower reels between, as seen in Fig 2.5. These reels are convex, but slope sharply away from a central peak.

Buds or husks interspersed with beads are a further variation (Fig 2.39). One end of the bud is quarter-spherical; the petal ends are formed with curving cuts up to the centerline, sometimes with an "eye" at the junction between the petals (Fig 2.40). The eye is made by stabbing in a small circle and then "drilling" by twirling the gouge between the palms. Some hint of modeling can be achieved with a few strokes of a deep gouge (veiner). For further variety, leaves can be overlapped, and eyes can be placed alternately on either side of the profile.

Fig 2.41 shows a simple variation on the basic bead and billet, in which an additional bead is formed within the billet.

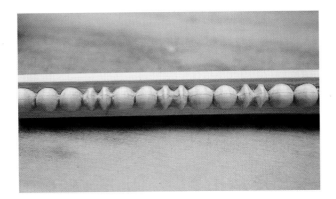

*Fig 2.38  Bead and reel*

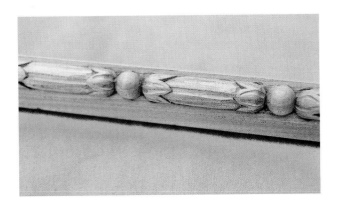

*Fig 2.39  Small astragal carved with buds or husks*

*Fig 2.41  Bead and billet with additional bead within the billet*

*Fig 2.40  Ovolo decorated with shell and dart, and husk astragal, Lenygon Collection (Colonial Williamsburg Foundation/ Frederick Wilbur)*

## SPIRALS

Because the astragal is half-round, the eye can be tricked into thinking that it is indeed round, with the rear part mysteriously hidden within the material. Beads at the edge of a board can be carried three-quarters of the way round, making the illusion easier to achieve. In the case of spiral designs this is certainly what is implied. Of course, there are some decorations to be found literally spiraling around columns and staircase balusters.

The simplest rendition is the **rope** or **cable** molding, which is a half-round spiraling around a half-round. Figs 2.50–2.52 all show the basic form, used in conjunction with various styles of ovolo. After marking the diagonals with a miter square or a 45° template, use a parting tool to begin the valleys. A gouge in an inverted position then serves to round over the strands of rope (Figs 2.42 and 2.43). Sometimes a few deep gouge cuts at the extremities are used to emphasize the flow or twist of the strands (see Figs 2.50 and 2.51). Similar to this are spiraling bands infilled with beads (Fig 2.44), and continuous twists of leaves. Sometimes a rod in the center acts as a visual cue to pronounce the intended spiral (Fig 2.45). After the spiral has been set in, the rod is defined by a straight chisel placed on either side of the centerline. In order for the ribbon to appear to flow behind the rod, the relieving of the surface behind the rod should take on a dished shape. Another common motif is the ribbon spiraling around a central cylinder infilled with flower blossoms, as described in the next section. The spiral or interlaced

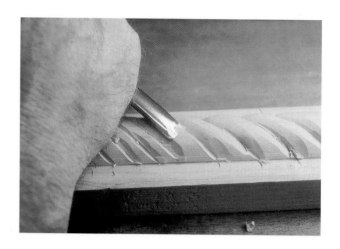

Fig 2.42 Rope molding: the strands have been separated with the V-tool, and the inverted gouge is now beginning to round them over

Fig 2.43 Partially completed rope molding (see Figs 2.50–2.52 for finished examples)

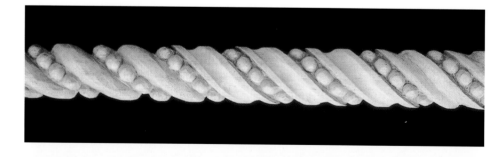

Fig 2.44 Spiral with beads

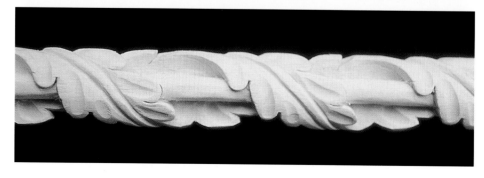

Fig 2.45 Spiral leaves, with central rod

Fig 2.46  Single ribbon and flower

ribbons isolate the flowers to create the repeat, while at the same time giving the element continuity. Rarely are flowers themselves strung along the length.

It is easier to work spiral designs if the molding is shaped as a half-round without any grounding or fillets, and then mounted on a backing board for carving. Raising the molding from the bench top allows the sides to be fully modeled. When complete, the molding can be mounted either on the surface of the structure or in a recess.

## Ribbon and flower

As Figs 2.31, 2.46, and 2.47 illustrate, there are many possibilities for combining the flower blossom and the ribbon. To carve these sorts of designs, the ribbon is first laid out and then the spaces filled in with flower and half-flower designs. After marking the centerline, the diagonal edges of the ribbon are established. A piece of cardboard cut to the width of the intended ribbon can be used to lay out the diagonals. A single twist of ribbon creates a parallelogram as in Fig 2.46; the flower in this case, of course, has to have petals of differing lengths in order to fill the parallelogram-shaped area. As an alternative, two ribbons can criss-cross along the astragal to create vesica piscis or lozenge shapes with triangles on the sides, which then can hold a more regularly shaped flower (see Figs 2.31 and 2.47); this is a variation of the guilloche, described above. The ribbon is usually made to look rippled, in which case the edges need to echo each other in their undulation. Shaping the ribbon in a long sweep along the side of the astragal will enhance the illusion that it passes behind the cylinder.

The flowers should be set in first, before any relieving is done; then relieve the ground between flower

Fig 2.47  Double ribbon (vesica piscis) and flower, Lenygon Collection (Colonial Williamsburg Foundation/ Frederick Wilbur)

and ribbon. As with most moldings, the ground should echo the shape of the original profile. Modeling of the ribbon consists of grooves running along the length of the molding from one edge of the ribbon to the other, matching the undulations in the shape of the edge; these grooves can be made randomly deeper on one side or the other. The flower centers are set in and relieved so that the petals appear to come out from behind them; then the center is rounded over. Model each petal with a single shallow gouge cut, emphasizing the downward slope toward the center. To give the petals more interest, three or four deep veins can be made from about the middle of the petal to the central disk; these should not be fussy cuts, but slight variations add character and interest. On this type of molding, stippling or punching of the background serves to emphasize the separate elements.

# THE OVOLO MOLDING

The ovolo is a convex molding whose profile may vary from a quarter-round to a quarter-ellipse, with or without a quirk between the convex surface and the projecting fillet above; Fig 2.48 shows some characteristic ovolo sections.

The design most commonly used to decorate the ovolo profile is the **egg and dart** (Fig 2.49); though, as Figs 2.50 to 2.52 show, many other designs have also been found appropriate for use on this versatile molding. Occasionally, leaves of various kinds are carved across the run of the molding (see the backband of the mantelpiece in Fig 2.3).

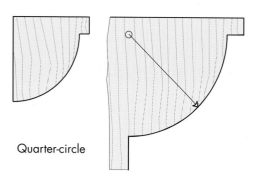
Quarter-circle

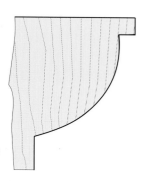

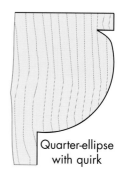
Quarter-ellipse

Quarter-ellipse with quirk

Fig 2.48  Molding profiles: the ovolo

Fig 2.49  Ovolo with large egg and dart

Fig 2.51  Trefoil decoration with rope astragal, Blandfield, Caret, VA (1769) (by courtesy of Mrs James C. Wheat)

Fig 2.50  Flower and shell with rope astragal, Lenygon Collection (Colonial Williamsburg Foundation/Frederick Wilbur)

Fig 2.52  Flower ovolo with rope astragal

## Egg and dart

The orientation of egg and dart is perpendicular to the length of the molding, and this gives it some distinctive characteristics. The quarter-circle or quarter-ellipse profile of the ovolo more or less dictates a similar shape in its carved elements: hence the half-elliptical "basket" holding an egg. This basket is common to all the variations, whether it holds eggs or shells or flowers. The baskets can be separated by a fairly literal depiction of a dart, or they can be connected with a short band. The dart is often simplified to a "tongue" (Fig 2.53) or a pointed petal (Fig 2.54). The egg and dart needs to be laid out with particular care because of the bold shapes it contains.

Egg and dart is usually laid off from the center of the run of molding, with either dart or basket in the middle. The most visible length should be symmetrical; the shorter lengths can be manipulated to make the corners appear to work out well. Some moldings are matched at the outside miters and allowed to run as they will into inside corners, but egg and dart requires attention at both ends. When working with different lengths, it is extremely unlikely that the design will always split nicely in the middle of an egg to make the corner symmetrical. Stretching or compressing the design might make the overall effect visibly jarring when compared to adjacent pieces. Some solution has to be found for this awkward juxtaposition. In quality work, a half-leaf is carved on each side of the miter, so the joint is "covered" by a leaf. The egg and dart appears to continue under the leaf, and the eye is tricked into seeing an uninterrupted design (Figs 2.55 and 2.56).

Fig 2.55 Egg and dart with corner leaf

Fig 2.53 Egg and tongue

Fig 2.54 Simple egg and dart

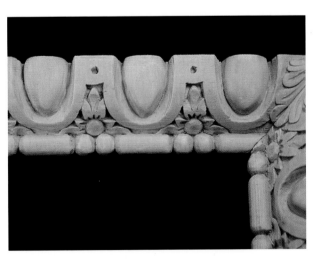

Fig 2.56 Egg and flower with corner leaf. Note that, because the two moldings in this case are of different lengths, the miters fall in different places: the horizontal piece is mitered at the egg, the vertical at the flower

An increment has to be found which allows a pleasing plumpness to the egg—though in historical examples there is wide variation in the relationship of egg to basket and of basket width to the width of the ovolo. The basket is generally an elliptical shape. In the literal interpretation, space is needed between baskets in order to carve the shaft for the dart.

Lay out your practice piece (Figs 2.57 and 2.58) and decide on the tools which are likely to be required. Remember that, because the basket is elliptical, the bottom curve will be of smaller radius than the upper sides as they reach the back (or upper) fillet. (It is easier to carve the egg without the upper fillet, but usually smaller moldings are machined as one piece.)

Fig 2.57 Carving sequence: using a metal pattern to lay out the eggs

Fig 2.58 Using a metal pattern for the corner leaf

## Carving the egg and dart

Begin with a #5 or #7 at the bottom of the basket; the tool chosen depends on the narrowness of the elliptical basket. Place the gouge right on the junction of the ovolo and the flat ground (or backing board), or on the edge of the quirk between the ovolo and its associated astragal. The angle of the gouge should be slightly higher than perpendicular to the ovolo. (In some eighteenth-century examples the basket is so wide that the two sides don't actually meet at the ground, but seem to plunge under it.) With the same tool or an appropriately shallower one, overlap the previous cut and work up toward the upper fillet. For instance, a #7 might be used at the bottom and a #5 to extend the basket to the top fillet. Setting in both sides in this way defines the outside of the basket (Fig 2.59).

Next, set in the "flares" or wings at the tip of the dart. Mark the upper extent of the flares with a pencil marking gauge or with the gauge block described earlier, and then stab in with a #7 on either side of the dart centerline at about a 45° angle, so that the width of the edge of the gouge fits between the ground at the bottom and the edge of basket (Fig 2.60). Clean out the resulting triangular piece, setting in again as necessary. This ground should be parallel to the back of the molding (that is, parallel to the wall when the molding is in position), which means cleaning out the deep corners. Good light helps here. If an astragal is attached, a shallow frontbent gouge is handy to extricate the triangular piece and smooth the ground (Figs 2.61 and 2.62). The basket at this point can be slightly undercut. Because the valleys on either side of the dart shaft are

Fig 2.59 Setting in the basket with a #5 gouge: the initial cut at the base is being extended toward the upper fillet

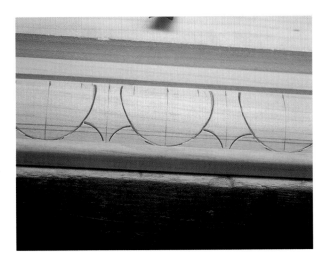

Fig 2.60 Baskets and flares of darts set in

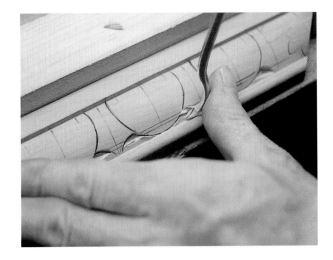

Fig 2.61 Grounding between dart and basket with a shallow frontbent gouge

Fig 2.62 The grounding completed

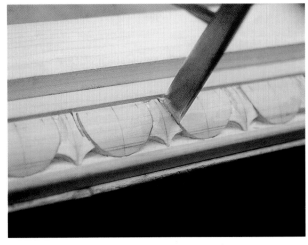

Fig 2.63 Carving the dart: the flares have been beveled on either side, and the valleys are being set in

quite deep, it is good to have as much material to the basket side as possible for strength, and this is why the dart is done before the egg—no conundrum here!

To shape the dart itself, first bevel off the two flares below the level of the basket perimeter. Then, alternating between the #5 gouge that defined the basket and a straight chisel, form the valleys on either side of the dart shaft (Fig 2.63). Before reaching full depth, define the inside or backside of the flares by stabbing in with a narrower #7, parallel to the front edge of the flare (these stab cuts can be seen clearly on the left-hand dart in Fig 2.64); then return to the chisel to work the valley down to its full depth. Use a skew chisel to make the various planes join crisply. As before, it is perfectly acceptable for the perimeter of the basket to

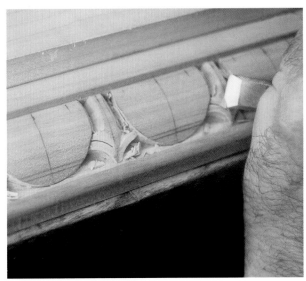

Fig 2.64 Using the chisel to form the valleys

be undercut slightly. Try to place the tools identically each time in order to maintain continuously smooth surfaces (Fig 2.65).

The inside of the basket slopes in to meet the egg, so do not set in vertically with stabbing cuts, but angle the tools so as to create a valley. Work downward from the top of the molding toward the tip of the egg. Usually this valley is started with the same #5 gouge as was used to set in the outside perimeter of the basket. As you work down the egg from top to bottom, the front surface of the basket decreases in width, making more room for the egg (which of course is decreasing in width as well). If the molding is viewed straight from the top, a smooth ellipse should be seen. As the valley is worked down, the surface of the egg can also be shaped by turning over the gouge and rounding the form so as to echo the outside shape of the basket (Figs 2.66 and 2.67). A smaller #7 can be used to form the narrow end of the egg. The shape of the egg as it meets the back fillet should be semicircular. It does not

matter if the eggs lie slightly below the original profile of the ovolo, as long as they are all even. Finally, to soften the straplike effect of the basket rim the surface can be slightly hollowed (this can be seen very clearly in Fig 2.49). The completed molding is shown in Figs 2.68 and 2.69.

*Fig 2.66 Beginning to form the valley between egg and basket*

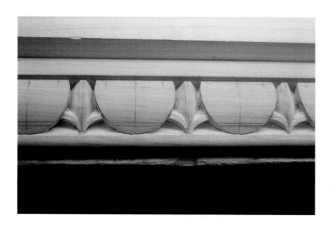

*Fig 2.65 The darts completed: uniformity is all-important*

*Fig 2.67 Rounding the egg with an inverted gouge*

*Fig 2.68 Completed molding, with the basket edges slightly fluted*

Fig 2.69  *Multiple lengths of bolection molding for door panels*

## GADROONING

This term describes a protruding profile of elliptical ovolo or three-quarter nosed section which is carved with rope-like lobes and valleys sweeping diagonally toward a back fillet. The lobes are sometimes separated by smaller lobes or flutes bordered by fillets (Figs 2.70 and 2.71). It does not seem to be a common decoration in Greek architecture, but was widely used in the Renaissance and after. More generally, the term is used for any series of lobe-like decorations, such as is often found in other situations, particularly turnings of the Tudor period. At times the gadrooned molding serves as a **necking** on pilasters (as in Fig 2.1), as an edge treatment on tables and chest lids, or on chair rails (Figs 2.72 and 2.73). Like the rope molding, it is usually laid out so that the direction of the carving is split along a centerline running toward opposite ends. The table apron in Fig 2.72 shows both a rope molding and gadrooning. Carving the molding is described in Chapter 7 (pages 149–51).

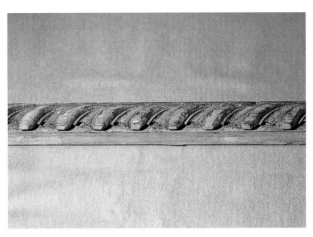

Fig 2.71  *Gadrooning with flutes and fillets, Lenygon Collection (Colonial Williamsburg Foundation/Frederick Wilbur)*

Fig 2.72  *Gadrooning on upper edge of table (with rope motif on lower edge), c.1761–71 (Colonial Williamsburg Foundation/Frederick Wilbur)*

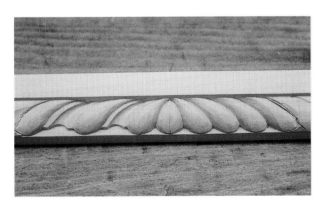

Fig 2.70  *Two types of gadroon: one plain and one with alternating flutes and fillets*

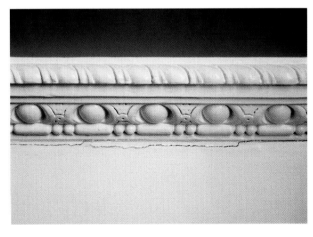

Fig 2.73  *Gadrooning on chair rail, Hammond–Harwood House, Annapolis, MD (Hammond–Harwood House Association/Frederick Wilbur)*

## THE TORUS MOLDING

The final profile to be discussed here is the torus, which is a large half-round, usually associated with the Ionic and Corinthian column base. It can be decorated with bundled reeds, leaves wrapped with ribbons, complex guilloche designs, and sometimes with acanthus leaves perpendicular to the run, as in Fig 2.74. Because it is difficult to fabricate a circular blank, as for a column base, without end grain (unless quite large), this element in its traditional form is not often carved in wood. In Fig 2.74, and in the example described in Chapter 7, the torus molding is wrapped around a square post, so avoiding this difficulty.

## THE FRIEZE

The frieze is specifically a part of the entablature of the orders, as explained in Chapter 1, but the term can be used for any wide band set off by smaller moldings. It often is an element of door architraves, mantelpieces, and furniture of classical design. It can be plain, or decorated with shallow fret-like designs; it can imitate the Doric frieze with flutes and rosettes, or be carved in high relief with, for example, a procession of animals and humans. The frieze is often decorated with **anthemion** (see Figs 2.5 and 3.34) or palmette (Fig 2.75), or with garlands of flowers or swags of drapery (see Fig 7.25).

*Fig 2.74 Torus molding with acanthus leaves, carved in stone, Virginia General Assembly Building, Richmond, VA*

Friezes can be **pulvinated** or convex in section; in this case the profile is only a segment of a circle, and not a half-round like the torus. This profile can be left plain or decorated with bundled reeds, oak or laurel leaves; more often than not these are "wrapped" by ribbons (Figs 2.76 and 2.77). Fig 2.78 shows a bundle of reeds which, if mounted horizontally, would be a pulvinated frieze; but this was in fact carved as a vertical pilaster. More about carving the pulvinated frieze is explained in Chapter 7.

*Fig 2.75 Palmette decoration on pulvinated frieze, with bead and billet astragal*

Fig 2.76 Pulvinated frieze
on table, Victoria and
Albert Museum (V&A
Museum/Frederick Wilbur)

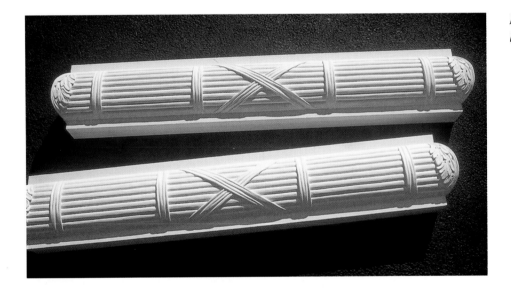

Fig 2.77 Friezes of
bundled reeds

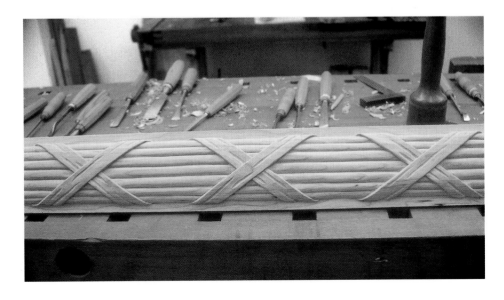

Fig 2.78 Reeded pilaster

C H A P T E R

# MOLDINGS II

Concave moldings • The cyma profiles • Foliage

## CONCAVE MOLDINGS

The general term **cove** means a concave profile or section (Fig 3.1). The **cavetto**, more specifically, is at least a quarter-circle or quarter-ellipse in profile and is used primarily to provide a contrast with protruding moldings such as astragals and ovolos. On picture frames a large cavetto, either plain or fluted, serves to draw the viewer into the picture. The cavetto can also serve as a **bed molding**, which is used as a transition between frieze and corona in the entablature. The **congé** is a quarter-ellipse which eases into a flatter plane and is usually "stopped" at its bottom edge by an astragal or fillet; it serves as a cornice molding and is decorated with upright leaves. It is also called the *Egyptian gorge,* as most Egyptian temple cornices are of this configuration. The **scotia** is a deeply concave shape, usually configured using arcs of two different radii. It is associated with Ionic column bases,

Omnis ars naturae
imitatio est.

*All art is but imitation
of nature.*

SENECA

where it separates the two tori, and forms the "waist" of urns and other such shapes.

The cove is rarely carved, simply because shadow would obscure the carved decoration. There is also the practical difficulty of manipulating straight-edged gouges on a concave surface, where the tool does not cut the deepest part as much as the sloping sides.

Obviously, if the cove is shallow or large enough, carving can be done, and examples will often be found. Guilloche (see Fig 3.3) and interlaced ribbons and flowers are two such possibilities. Much more common are stiff leaves or flutes oriented perpendicularly to the run of the cove; this decoration is used in cornices and other places where the ornament is above the viewer, as on the door entablature shown in Fig 3.2.

The approach to carving the shallow cavetto is similar to that used for convex moldings: marking a centerline and increments, and using a metal pattern to

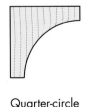

Quarter-circle

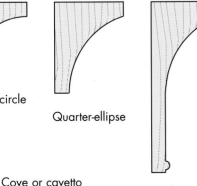

Quarter-ellipse

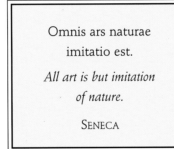

Cove or cavetto

Congé

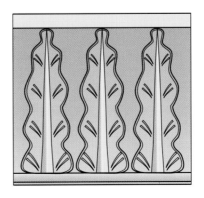

Stiff-leaf ornament on congé

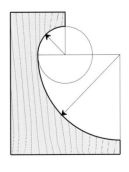

Scotia

*3.1 The concave profiles*

53

*Fig 3.2 Flutes carved in cavetto of entablature, Hammond–Harwood House, Annapolis, MD (Hammond–Harwood House Association/ Frederick Wilbur)*

transfer the overall shape of the design. The depth of relief should be consistent throughout the width of the molding; that is, the ground should echo the original curve of the molding. This means that one should anticipate that the edges of the molding will be cut away, which will alter the relationship with bordering surfaces (Fig 3.3).

## THE CYMA PROFILES

The reversing curve, combining the projection of an astragal with the concavity of the cavetto, gives the family of moldings generally called **ogees.** This shape lends itself to the rendition of foliage (but not many other motifs) better than the previously discussed moldings, since the S-shaped profile echoes the inherent flow of leaves carved perpendicular to the run. *Ogee* is a term used for any reversing curve, whether in profile, plan, or elevation, from a small molding to a huge Gothic arch. In classical terminology, moldings with this profile are classified as **cyma recta** and **cyma reversa** (see Fig 3.4*a*). The difference between them depends on their orientation to the viewer and their relationship to adjacent fillets, though the actual reversing curves may be of the same size and profile.

*Fig 3.3 Shallow cove with guilloche and flower pattern; it is important to maintain a uniform depth of ground*

## CYMA RECTA

The cyma recta or Doric cyma is concave at its outer extent and convex at its back. The cymatium of a cornice is usually a cyma recta (though it can also be an ovolo or cavetto). The cymatium of the door entablature in Fig 3.2 is a cyma recta. The feel of the molding is one of reaching or projecting, and the visual effect is one of lightness.

## CYMA REVERSA

In the cyma reversa or Lesbian cyma, the convexity is foremost and the concavity is at the back. The feeling is that it is a supportive member, and it is used in console blocks, in the bed molding of the Ionic order, and for panel (**bolection**) moldings in doors, as well as in door and window architraves. (Fig 7.1 portrays a typical eighteenth-century architrave.)

## DRAWING THE CYMA PROFILES

The profile of both varieties is not literally an S-curve consisting of two semicircles, but is made of two arcs forming a sinuous line—anything from two quarter-circles to shallower arcs, including asymmetrical combinations of arcs. See Fig 2.6 for a comparison of Greek and Roman versions, based respectively on elliptical and circular arcs. It is possible to use the modern "Roman ogee" router bit to create the molding (this is actually a cyma recta profile, as the fillet is at the top of the bit), but the arcs are a little deep. (See Fig 3.9 for a waterleaf carved on this profile.) At the other extreme, the cyma profile on modern door casings is too shallow to give much definition to foliage carving. Cymas that are quirked—that is, have a deep valley between fillet and profile—are acceptable for acanthus foliage, but difficult for waterleaf. As explained below, the valley between leaves flares and deepens as it meets the fillet, and the extra depth of the quirk makes for an acute angle which is difficult to clean up.

To draw a symmetrical cyma curve to fit a specific space, first make allowance for any fillet, then draw a square or rectangle of the available size. Using a rectangle will make the profile shallower. Now draw the

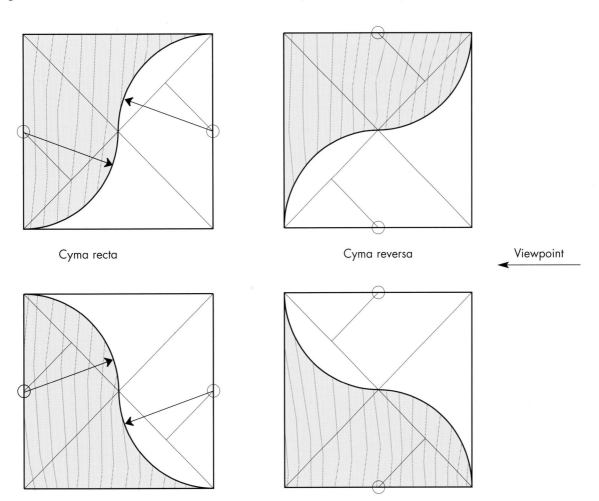

Cyma recta

Cyma reversa

Viewpoint

*Fig 3.4  The cyma profiles* (a) *Symmetrical profiles drawn within a square*

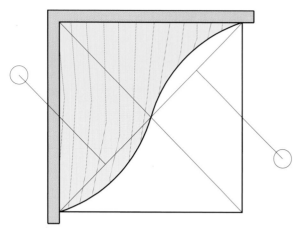
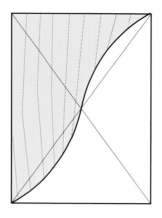
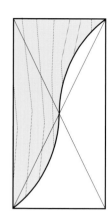

(b) *Profiles drawn with shallower arcs, and within rectangles*

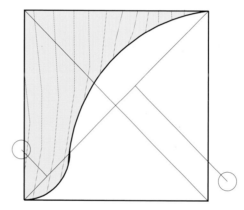

(c) *Asymmetrical profile obtained by dividing the diagonal off-center*

*Fig 3.4 (continued)*

diagonals; the point where they cross marks the transition between the concave and convex sections of the profile. Bisect each segment and draw lines perpendicular to one of the diagonals. By using the point of intersection of this perpendicular with the side of the square, draw arcs from each corner to the intersection of the diagonals. All four of the profiles shown in Fig 3.4*a* are constructed in this way. Placing the center of the arc further from or closer to the diagonal makes the cyma respectively shallower or deeper; using an increasingly narrower rectangle will accomplish the same effect (Fig 3.4*b*). An asymmetrical profile can be drawn by dividing the diagonal off-center instead of bisecting it (Fig 3.4*c*).

## CARVING THE WATERLEAF

The simplest decoration associated with the cyma reversa is the waterleaf, which is a series of leaves connected *ad infinitum*, as the circular picture frame of Fig 3.5 illustrates. The leaves can be simply tongue-like forms (Figs 3.5 and 3.6), or more integrated with each other as in Figs 3.7 and 3.8. (The somewhat larger leaf and dart mentioned below can be very similar, and is

often confused with waterleaf.) The individual leaves are separated by a rounded space—not exactly an eye—and have identical tips, which may be either a simple intersection of arcs, or an ogee point as in Fig 3.9. The undulating surface is accentuated by the widely flaring "vein" in the middle of each leaf. Most often there is a secondary layer of leaves of which only the tips are seen. Further variations are shown in Fig 3.10. On almost all cyma foliage the leaves "sprout" from the convex side and flow into the concave side as if reaching for sunlight.

The marking wheel can be used to lay out the increments, as only unit lines perpendicular to the run are needed. This molding is easy to lay out correctly at the miters, because the units are small and it is no trouble to "stretch" half a dozen repeats. A line parallel to the run may be desired in order to mark the circular divisions or "eyes" between leaves. Mark the unit and half-unit lines. A rectangular piece of metal pattern stock can be used as a sort of try square, slid along the molding in order to mark these increments. Indicate the leaf tips by a penciled "v", so they cannot be inadvertently confused with the circular separations.

*Fig 3.5 Picture frame with continuous row of waterleaf (by courtesy of Thomas A. Goddard)*

*Fig 3.6 Simple waterleaf, with acanthus leaf on the cyma recta above, Lenygon Collection (Colonial Williamsburg Foundation/Frederick Wilbur)*

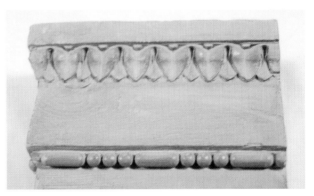

*Fig 3.7 A more elaborate form with two layers of leaves, and bead and billet astragal below, Lenygon Collection (Colonial Williamsburg Foundation/Frederick Wilbur)*

*Fig 3.8 Lid of Flemish chest, Victoria and Albert Museum: an elaborate form of waterleaf above, with bead and billet astragal and foliage frieze below (V&A Museum/ Frederick Wilbur)*

*Fig 3.9 Waterleaf on routed molding, showing ogee curves to tips of leaves*

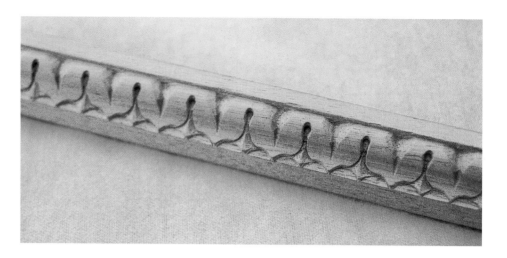

With an appropriate gouge, stab the semicircular space between leaf points, and then relieve with a flat (preferably fishtail) gouge to isolate the leaf tip (Fig 3.11). Next, stab in the circular division or eye with a quick gouge to establish the separation of the leaves. With the same gouge as before, but held the opposite way, stab in the reversed curve toward the circular division, creating an ogee-shaped leaf on either side of the midline. A smaller, flat gouge may be needed to complete the line up to the eye. All main elements are now complete and further modeling can be done. Relieve the secondary leaf and work the midline peak into the eye (Fig 3.12). Work the flaring V-shaped vein into the primary leaf (Fig 3.13). The molding can be considered complete at this point, or a simple modeling can be added as shown in Fig 3.14. This type of waterleaf is usually a secondary molding and should be kept simple and crisp with the minimum of modeling.

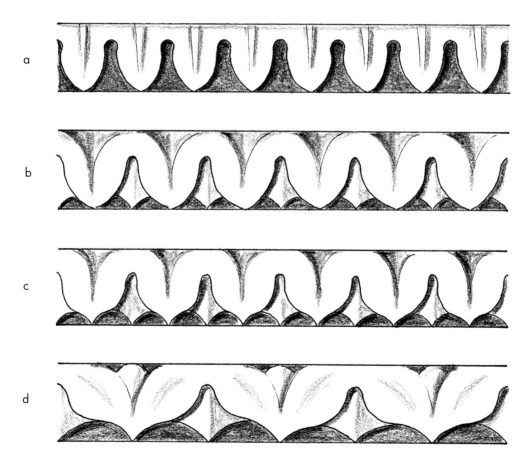

*Fig 3.10 Some typical waterleaf patterns, in order of increasing complexity*

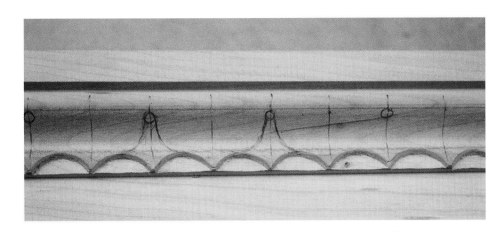

Fig 3.11 Carving sequence: the spaces between leaf tips have been set in and grounded out

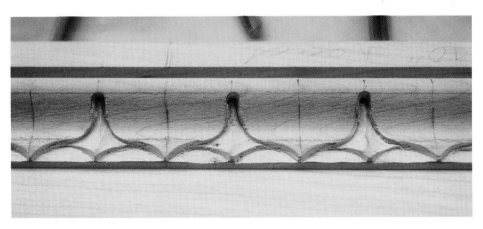

Fig 3.12 The secondary leaves set in and their surfaces beveled

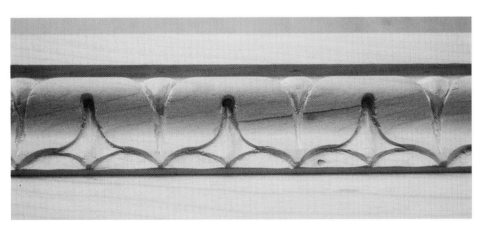

Fig 3.13 The central vein defined

Fig 3.14 Modeling on the surface of the leaf is an optional extra

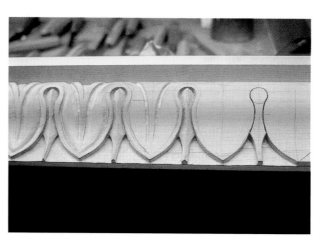

Fig 3.15 Leaf and dart, with rope astragal, on a mantel at the Hammond–Harwood House, Annapolis, MD (Hammond–Harwood House Association/Frederick Wilbur)

Fig 3.16 Stages in carving the leaf and dart

Fig 3.17 Partially finished leaf and dart

The **leaf and dart**, heart and dart, or leaf and tongue (Figs 3.15–3.17), is similar to the waterleaf described above in that it has an abstract quality to it, though it has more depth and presents less flow along its length, having something of the perpendicularity of egg and dart. The top molding on the Erechtheion cornice in Fig 2.5 is of this design; notice that when deeply modeled this molding looks similar to the egg and dart below.

## FOLIAGE

As one complicates this basic leaf by adding more leaflets or lobes to it, the design begins to portray a more realistic leaf. Figs 3.18–3.20 show a selection of progressively more complicated treatments; Fig 3.21 is a typical variation. Often several different foliage moldings are used adjacent to each other: Fig 3.22, for example, shows a waterleaf with an acanthus leaf, and 3.23 shows a leaf and dart with an acanthus.

The most common multi-lobed designs derive from the acanthus plant indigenous to the Mediterranean area. There are two species of the acanthus—*Acanthus spinosus* and *A. mollis*—and, as Fig 3.24 shows, *Acanthus spinosus* has a sharply pointed leaf, crinkly and ragged and presenting many different planes. The leaflets have deep valleys which cause the edges to undulate steeply, and it is these two characteristics which are emphasized in the surface modeling of the leaf. There

Fig 3.18 Stages in making
a lobed leaf with punched
background

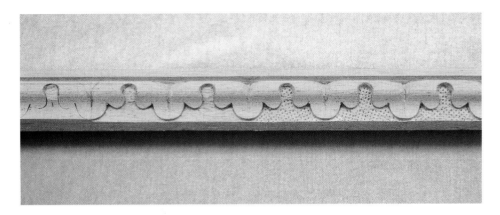

Fig 3.19 Stages in making
a more complex lobed leaf

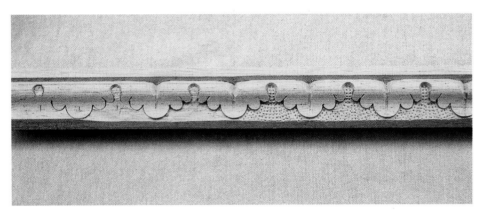

Fig 3.20 Stages in making
a small complex leaf

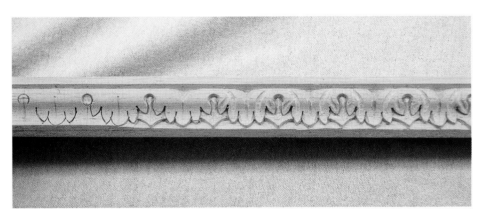

Fig 3.21 Acanthus-like leaf with prominent secondary
leaves, and rope astragal, Lenygon Collection (Colonial
Williamsburg Foundation/Frederick Wilbur)

Fig 3.22 Acanthus and waterleaf, Lenygon Collection
(Colonial Williamsburg Foundation/Frederick Wilbur)

*Fig 3.23 Acanthus and leaf and dart, carved in stone, Virginia General Assembly Building, Richmond, VA*

*Fig 3.24* Acanthus spinosus *in real life*

is a pattern in the chaos, however, and the natural leaf can be regularized easily. The Greek version used on Corinthian capitals and brackets is of this variety (see Figs 6.66 and 6.67). The Romans tended to prefer the rounded lobes of *Acanthus mollis*. The drawings in Fig 3.25 show the natural *Acanthus spinosus* and some examples of its adaptation both to vertical decoration as on a Corinthian capital and to horizontal decoration as on moldings. It can also be used in combination with C or S scrolls.

This ubiquitous motif has been stylized more than any other, showing up on all sorts of objects from silverware to glazed tiles, from manuscript borders to their ivory covers, being simplified on one hand and contorted almost beyond recognition on the other. The acanthus **rinceau,** in which swirls of leaves create spiral patterns, first appeared in Roman architecture and subsequently became a favorite Renaissance motif for

friezes and panels. This free-flowing adaptation was one of the inspirations for the baroque carvings of Grinling Gibbons, of which Fig 3.26 shows a typical example. Moldings came to reflect this enthusiasm, and the rigid orientation of the leaf was liberated as the moldings swirled and curled like those in Figs 3.27–3.30. There are many examples in which the sweep of foliage is on an angle, and often groups of flowers and leaves combine to make an isolated (though repeated) composition. Sometimes leaves even intertwine from group to group.

The motif was easily transplanted to pieces of furniture—a fire screen, a pier-glass frame, and a chair leg are shown in Figs 3.31, 3.32, and 3.33. In Chapter 4 a selection of brackets which feature an acanthus on their front elevations is illustrated, and in Chapter 6 the procedure for carving a pilaster capital with acanthus leaves will be discussed.

There are other leaves to be found in classical ornament: olive, laurel, ivy, grape, and oak. The oak and laurel are common on pulvinated friezes (see Fig 7.3). Another of the most popular plant motifs among the Greeks was the **anthemion.** It is thought to be a combination of the palmette and the honeysuckle, connected by S-scrolls. The anthemion is found around the necks of columns, on friezes and cymatia (Fig 3.34). (We have already seen a fine example from the Erechtheion in Fig 2.5.) This motif was revived and used extensively in the later Adam style. The anthemion requires a relatively flat ground or profile to make it effective, and is more of a relief carving than a molding decoration.

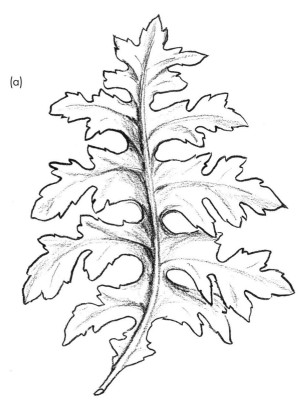

(a)

*Fig 3.25 Some of the many possible treatments of acanthus foliage: (a) near natural, (b) vertical and (c) horizontal adaptations, and (d) sprouting from volute*

*Fig 3.26 Grinling Gibbons, decoration in St Paul's Cathedral, London: the acanthus at its most exuberant*

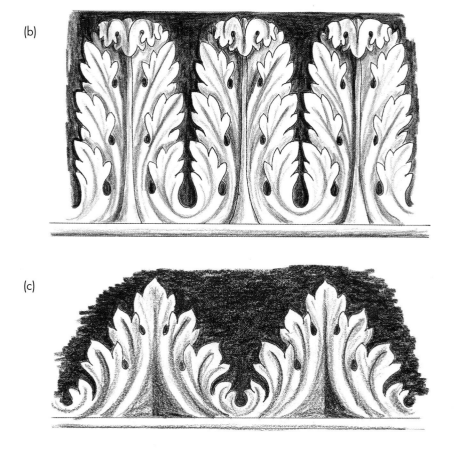

(b)

(c)

(d)

Fig 3.27  Picture frame with acanthus and flowers (by courtesy of Thomas A. Goddard)

Fig 3.28  Foliage molding on a fragment from the Lenygon Collection (Colonial Williamsburg Foundation/Frederick Wilbur)

Fig 3.29 Foliage molding with rinceau-like shapes, on a door architrave in the Victoria and Albert Museum (V&A Museum/Frederick Wilbur)

Fig 3.30  Foliage molding with curl in high relief, from the Lenygon Collection; note the simplified treatment of the area beneath the curl (Colonial Williamsburg Foundation/Frederick Wilbur)

Fig 3.31 *Acanthus scroll on eighteenth-century screen (Colonial Williamsburg Foundation/Frederick Wilbur)*

Fig 3.32 *Acanthus on pier-glass frame*

Fig 3.33 *Acanthus on chair leg (Colonial Williamsburg Foundation/Frederick Wilbur)*

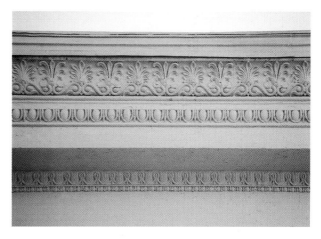

Fig 3.34 *Anthemion on cymatium, with egg and dart and leaf and dart below, at the University of Virginia, Charlottesville*

The conventionalized acanthus leaf usually has a prominent center stem or vein, and the stems of the side leaves curve out from it (see Fig 3.25a). The side leaves are made up of a central pointed lobe (or a rounded "Roman" lobe) and a number of smaller lobes of similar shape on either side. These side leaves usually overlap one another in succession, as if they have been bunched together, and create a teardrop-shaped "eye" between them. The side leaflets become smaller as they approach the tip of the main leaf. On Corinthian capitals or brackets—or indeed almost everywhere else—the tips of the leaves curl outward from the ground.

## Carving the acanthus molding

In this rendition of the foliage molding, the intention is to give the leaf an uncluttered formality. The cyma reversa profile is combined with a bead to allow the tips of the leaves to curl away from the cyma background. The spots of light created by the curling leaves make the linear quality of the molding more interesting. Often the prominent curves of the molding are given more modeling in order to catch the light, while the concave areas under the curls are not modeled at all, but simply carry the shapes of the leaves from base to curl (see Fig 3.30).

To create a workable pattern, allowance must be made for the curvature of the profile and the curled leaf tip, as well as the spacing between elements. The problem of miters cutting through elements, as in egg and dart, is minimized here because the center stem is calculated to fall on the miter joint and the leaves spaced accordingly. The stretching or compression of the primary leaf will depend on the specific length of molding required. The exception is in very short returns, where a whole leaf will not fit after the half-units of the miters have been allowed for. In fudging the design around such returns, the frontal elevation should be kept in mind. The increments should appear to be evenly spaced on either side of the returns.

In the sequence shown here, the curl will not have much detail so it can be dealt with after the main part of the leaf has been drawn. Tape a piece of tracing paper over the profile, aligning the edge with the bottom edge of the molding, and draw a perpendicular line representing the middle of the leaf. The proportion between the width of leaf along the run and the height of leaf across the width of molding varies greatly in historical examples. The space between primary leaves can be left as clear ground or filled with a secondary layer of leaves (often of different appearance or size, as in Fig 3.23) or additional elements such as buds, shells, etc. (see Fig 3.39).

After the main part of the leaf has been designed, the curl should be considered. A pattern should now be made, and the units and half-units marked on the lengths of molding. Parallel markings should be made to locate the "eyes" and any other salient features of the design.

The first stage of carving is to isolate the curl so the leaves below can be set in. The astragal between the curls should be cut away, using either a back saw or simply a series of stop-cuts with the chisel. Waste the bead down to the cyma profile, making sure that the acute corner created by the machining of the bead is carved away. This molding is set in and grounded like any other, but it is a good idea to "drill" the eyes first (with a #9 gouge spun between the palms) because it is easy to locate these accurately (Fig 3.35). It may be necessary to set in and ground in several stages so as to gain sufficient depth to allow for modeling of overlapping leaves, but, as in any relief, it is important to avoid making the side walls irregular or fuzzy. Enough depth must be obtained to make the leaves readily identifiable as such and to make them "pop" out or grow out of the background; otherwise they may look pasted on. There is no need for undercutting, however. Stabbing with #7 gouges ensures the leaflets have a nice curve to them (Fig 3.36). When modeling the leaf, the stem is first defined with a parting tool and then rounded with a turned-over gouge. The leaflets are then modeled with a shallow gouge (Fig 3.37) and given more definition with a veiner. These depressions should be carried down to the base of the molding, so that an undulating line is created at the bottom fillet or edge of the cyma (which will eventually be mounted against a background of some sort). Take care not to mar the fillet; you may need to clean up this plane with a flat chisel.

The curl is divided into three or more leaves, the central one of which comes to a point, while the leaflets to either side are wider. To create the impression of actually rolling over, a deep gouge is used from the side of the leaf to undercut the bead. (Figs 6.59–6.63 show this same undercutting technique.) To enhance this roll, the sides of the bead are rounded downward to either side so that the side leaflets appear lower than the main leaflet. The completed molding is shown in Fig 3.38. Fig 3.39 shows a slightly more elaborate leaf with a shell between repeats.

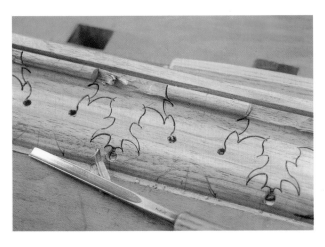

Fig 3.35 Carving sequence: initial setting in completed.
The eyes have been "drilled" with small gouges, and the
unwanted parts of the curl wasted away

Fig 3.37 Center vein formed, leaves being modeled with
shallow gouge

Fig 3.36 Final setting in and grounding completed

Fig 3.38 The completed molding

Fig 3.39 Partially
completed leaf and shell
molding

# CHAPTER 4

# VOLUTES

## Spiral, scroll, and volute • The voluted bracket

The spiral, scroll, and volute are similar geometric designs, and indeed the terms are often used interchangeably. As early as the treasury of Atreus of about 1325 BCE, the running spiral was carved as a surface decoration. So universal is the motif that it appears in nearly all art forms and in many media such as ironwork, silverware, ceramics, floral fabric patterns, and even on violins and other stringed instruments.

**Spiral** usually refers to a line which circles in (or out) about itself, as in grapevine tendrils or a climbing vine ascending a pole. It is a diminishing circle, or a circular form drawn using arcs with diminishing radii.

**Scroll** is a wider term for a sculptural configuration of the same idea. The C-scroll is a simple example. It consists of a curved form or body, usually with a combined convex and concave section, terminating in tight curls whose radius decreases

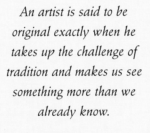

*An artist is said to be original exactly when he takes up the challenge of tradition and makes us see something more than we already know.*

DEMETRI PORPHYRIOS

slightly as the outline of the curl overlaps the concave part of the curved form (Fig 4.1). The sofa crest and the apron of the lowboy in Figs 4.2 and 4.3 show repetitions of this simple form strung together end to end. Note also that leaves seem to sprout from one of the curves on the lowboy. In fact, acanthus leaves are often configured to curl in C or S shapes. The console blocks of Fig 4.4 have a little more of a spiral to them, and are also fluted. If the form reverses itself so that the ends curl in opposite directions, an S-scroll is created, as in the table legs of Fig 4.5. The C and S scrolls, when cut out as silhouettes, often act as braces between the legs and apron of a table to soften the inherent harshness of the right angle. More commonly, they are used as borders or edge treatments for tables and panels.

The scroll is often used to represent paper, parchment, or other sheet goods which curl or roll up at the

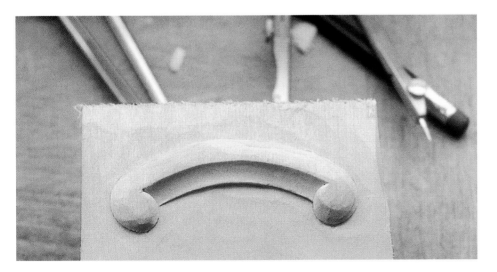

*Fig 4.1 The C-scroll in its simplest form*

*Fig 4.2 Composition of C-scrolls in the cresting of a sofa made in 1940 (by courtesy of Mrs Robert L. Wilbur)*

*Fig 4.3 C-scrolls and foliage on eighteenth-century table apron (Colonial Williamsburg Foundation/Frederick Wilbur)*

*Fig 4.4 C-scroll brackets*

*Fig 4.5 S-scroll and volute on eighteenth-century Italian table, Victoria and Albert Museum (V&A Museum/ Frederick Wilbur)*

corners. The **cartouche**, highly developed in the Renaissance, is a shield-shaped or oval tablet with a variously cut and scrolled perimeter. In the baroque and later periods the profusion and intermixing of geometric and botanical forms made the scroll something of a cliché.

**Volute** is more properly an architectural term used to describe the spiral which gives Ionic capitals their distinction, and which forms the primary element on various kinds of supporting brackets. And what is more supporting than a chair or table leg (Figs 4.6 and 4.7)? The volute is associated with many other elements: it is found on chair backs, on antefixae covering the ends of roof tiles, on acroteria at the corners and apex of a pediment, and under stair treads (Figs 4.8–4.11). It is used where a line needs to be terminated, as when a handrail reaches a newel post. In Fig 4.12, acanthus leaves themselves serve as the volute. The origin of the volute is probably vegetative; it is one of those archetypal motifs found in all cultures worldwide. There are many examples from nature, including mollusk shells (garden snail, nautilus), rams' horns, fiddlehead ferns, and vine tendrils—even the

*Fig 4.7  Table leg with floral volute, 1761–71 (Colonial Williamsburg Foundation/Frederick Wilbur)*

*Fig 4.6  Table leg with simple volute, 1755–70 (Colonial Williamsburg Foundation/Frederick Wilbur)*

*Fig 4.8  Chair back, 1876 (by courtesy of Mrs Robert L. Wilbur)*

71

structure of hurricanes, though it is doubtful that this influenced the ancient Greeks!

The architectural position and function of the voluted bracket determines its name: an **ancon** (Figs 4.13 and 4.14) is a bracket placed on a door or window facing or architrave to support the entablature or pediment above it. There are many uses for the **console** form, which by definition has a supporting function: mantel shelves, roof beams or cornices, porch roofs (Figs 4.15–4.21). Notice the range of configurations: Fig 4.16 is a simple geometric "Doric" console, while 4.17 has a floral garland hung from eye to eye; those of Fig 4.20 have a reversing sweep to the side elevation. When the bracket is placed on a wall to support a springing arch or vault rib, it is called a **corbel**. **Modillions** represent the ends of beams which support the upper cornice, and are found under the corona

*Fig 4.9 Antefix from the Parthenon, British Museum (British Museum/Frederick Wilbur)*

*Fig 4.10 Acroterion, University of Virginia*

*Fig 4.11 Stair bracket, Drayton Hall, Charleston, SC (Drayton Hall, a National Trust Historic Site/Frederick Wilbur)*

Fig 4.12  Acanthus volute,
University of Virginia

Fig 4.13  A typical ancon with S-shaped volute, 1820,
University of Virginia

Fig 4.14  An eighteenth-century ancon of more unorthodox
design, lacking the upper volute, Charleston, SC

*Fig 4.15 Mantelshelf console*

*Fig 4.16 A "Doric" bracket mimicking the Doric triglyph*

*Fig 4.17 Console with garland, Richmond, VA; note also the oval guilloche on the background frieze*

*Fig 4.18  Consoles with rosettes and plain leaf*

*Fig 4.19  Consoles with acanthus leaf, Chelsea, London*

*Fig 4.20  Ancons of "broken" silhouette, Chelsea, London*

Fig 4.21 *Ancon with volutes and foliage, and dentils above, Charleston, SC*

of the Corinthian order. They are placed horizontally (see Figs 1.8, 1.21, and 2.2), instead of vertically like the console block. **Keystones** of arches often take the form of a voluted bracket.

## THE VOLUTED BRACKET

The voluted bracket or console bracket has a side profile determined by a large volute flowing into an opposing smaller volute or a circle. Often the circle or volute contains a floral **rosette**, as shown in Figs 4.11, 4.18, and 4.21. The triangular space between the two elements may be filled with some sort of foliage sprouting from the volutes, as in Fig 4.13 amongst others, or with a group of flowers, as in 4.22. The face or front elevation is sometimes plainly modeled, decorated only with a center bead flanked by mirror-image cyma curves contained by edge fillets. The example to be described is of this type, and others can be seen in

Figs 4.16 and 4.17. Another common embellishment on the front surface is an acanthus leaf flowing from the larger to the smaller volute; the leaf tip often curls where it encounters the small roll or baluster which connects the two small side volutes (Fig 4.19).

Carving a volute may seem a daunting task; most cabinetmaking manuals either ignore the more sophisticated geometry or, if they do attempt it, the directions seem more complicated than necessary, or impractical for the situation. Carving small C and S scrolls by eye is fairly easy, but volutes require a little preparation. There is a particular need for accuracy when carving a larger piece such as a console bracket or an Ionic capital. There is nothing quite as jarring as when something meant to be regular isn't. Proper research is as important to competent carving as knowing wood properties or keeping gouges sharp.

Most instructions for drawing the volute are frustrating because they begin "given measurement *a*", or "with center at *c*", and one has the feeling that something crucial has been left out; or the instructions are based on the module, defined (as you will remember

Fig 4.22 *Consoles for a mantelpiece, with flowers and foliage*

from Chapter 1) as the diameter of the column just above its base. More often than not, on blueprints supplied by architect or millwork company the volute is indicated by squiggles and some measurements into which the bracket must be placed. The practical method described below starts from the overall space allowed for the bracket, to ensure that the volute drawn will fit.

There are two ways to produce a properly dimensioned volute: reduce or enlarge a pre-existing drawing on a photocopy machine, or mechanically draw one. Nearly always a photocopied design produces a stiff, lifeless, ill-fitting rendition of an inherently natural and flowing form—it is difficult to modify something that clearly was not originally designed for the space. There are a number of ways to draw the volute, and interested readers should consult the Select Bibliography (and see also Fig 6.6). Regardless of method, all volutes are based on a series of arcs with diminishing radii, the centers of which are established by constructing several concentric squares. The method I use is derived from Asher Benjamin's description in his *American Builder's Companion*, which is simple and versatile.

## DRAWING THE VOLUTE FOR A BRACKET

For the example, we shall assume that requirements dictate a bracket 4in (102mm) wide in front elevation by 11⅝in (295mm) tall, projecting from the background 4⅝in (117mm) in the side elevation (see Fig 4.24). On a sheet of drawing paper taped down flat, draw parallel lines, using a T-square, 4⅝in (117mm) apart to delimit the side elevation of the proposed bracket (Fig 4.23a). Remember that the volutes will be on the sides of the bracket. Draw a line perpendicular to these two parallels; this will form the centerline of the volute, so place it toward one side of the paper so that the rest of the bracket will fit. (The placement is not critical, as the length of the bracket will be measured from the volute after it has been drawn.)

Divide the space between the two parallel lines into eight equal units; the easiest way of doing this is to place a ruler diagonally across the two lines so that the zero mark falls on one line and the 8in mark (or the 160mm mark) on the other, then mark with the pencil at each inch mark (or every other centimeter mark) on the ruler. Using the T-square, draw parallels through each of these marks to meet the perpendicular line.

In the fifth space from what will be the front face of the bracket, and with its center on the perpendicular line, describe a circle whose diameter fits the space between the lines; this represents the eye of the volute. Your drawing should now look like Fig 4.23a. Using a set square with a 45° angle, draw a square inside this circle. Draw two further lines bisecting the sides of the square; these will, of course, pass through the center of the eye (Fig 4.23b). Divide these last two lines into six equal parts; this can be done accurately enough by eye. For the sake of clarity, this stage is shown enlarged on the right-hand side of Fig 4.23b. This gives the center points or loci of the spiraling arcs. (They are also the corner points of the concentric squares mentioned earlier, but we do not actually need to draw these in.)

Placing the fixed leg of the compass on point #1, begin by adjusting the marking leg about 1/16in (1.5mm) inside the parallel line designating the front face. (This small amount of waste is to allow for bandsawing the blank into a smooth curve.) Make an arc counterclockwise around to the invisible line extending from point #1 through point #2. Next, place the fixed leg on point #2 and continue the previously drawn arc, adjusting the radius inward to make a smooth transition of curvature (Fig 4.23c), as far as the line joining points #2 and #3. This procedure will carry the arcs to the opposite parallel line (representing the back edge), or slightly inside it. It will now be clear whether the volute will fit the available space or will run off the blank. If necessary, start again with a slightly smaller radius than before. It is important to avoid leaving a "flat" on the volute.

Continue placing the fixed leg on the points designated #3, #4, #5, etc., drawing a quarter of a circle each time, until you come up with something which looks like Fig 4.23d. Keep in mind that the compass must be adjusted each time to join smoothly with the previous arc. The last arc runs tangentially into the eye. Because of small inaccuracies in the drawing process, this sometimes does not occur gracefully, in which case a careful freehand adjustment will be needed. To draw a counterclockwise spiral, simply renumber the points in the opposite direction. Fig 4.24 shows the complete bracket whose volute we have just constructed.

In order to define the volute in three dimensions it must have some relief. In most cases the outer edge of the volute has a fillet or flat which slopes away from the eye and is defined by a cove or cavetto to the inside, or sometimes by a flute carved into the center of the fillet, as in the example to be described (see Figs 4.24, 4.38, and 4.39). The flutes are sometimes separated by astragals or a combination of astragals and fillets.

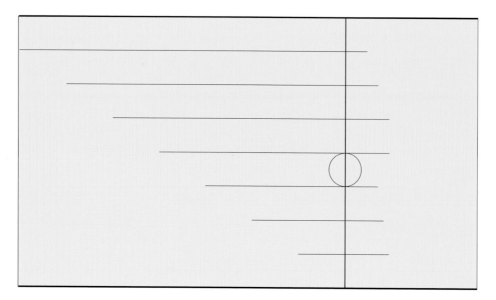

Fig 4.23 Stages in
drawing a volute
(a) The width of the
bracket is divided into eight
parts and the eye of the
volute inscribed in the fifth
space

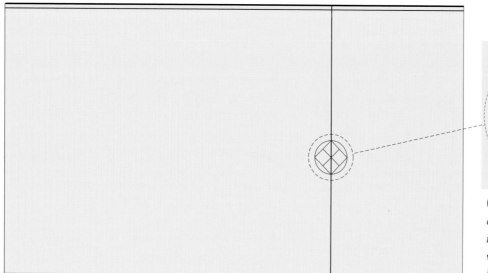

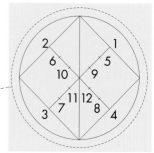

(b) A square (shown
enlarged at right) is
inscribed in the eye of the
volute, and the lines
bisecting the square are
divided into six equal parts

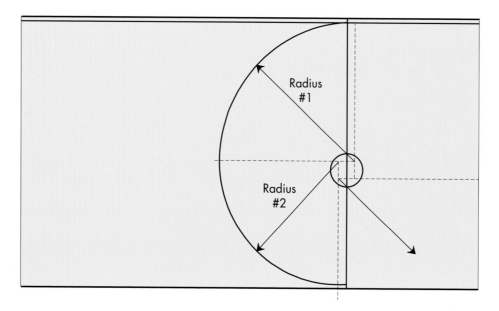

(c) The first two arcs have
been drawn in, centered
on points 1 and 2 within
the square

(d) *The completed spiral*

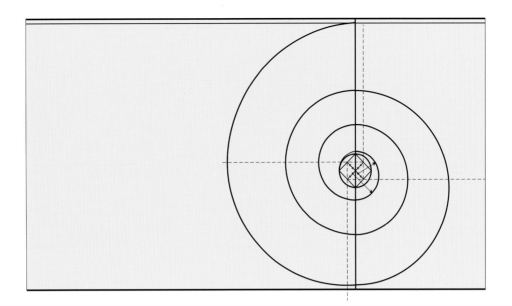

The capital from the Erechtheion (see Fig 6.10) shows shallow flutes separated by astragals. In our illustration the fillet decreases in width as it approaches the eye, so it is helpful to draw another spiral to assist in visualizing the relationships. This is done by the same procedure as above, except that the bisections of the square constructed in the eye are divided into five parts instead of six, thus moving the points in toward the center of the square. During the carving process this inner line will be carved away and will need to be redrawn using the outer spiral for reference. In historical examples the fillet sometimes remains the same width, only the cove decreasing as it spirals inward, but most commonly they decrease simultaneously.

There are many variations, as well, on the relationship between the two volutes which comprise a bracket, and frankly, there are historical examples which look absolutely terrible. A well-proportioned bracket goes something like this: the smaller volute is half the diameter of the larger, and the distance between the centers of the eyes is about two and a half times the diameter of the larger volute. The important thing—and one of the criteria by which the success of the design can be judged—is that the S-curve between the two volutes must be a smooth transition. This may be determined by the restrictions of space, and must therefore be sketched freehand. In later variations a step, or 90° interruption (see Fig 4.20), was often inserted to lengthen the bracket and/or to make the long curve visually more interesting. As the volutes are opposing spirals, the connection between the two is a cyma or reversing curve. The dimensions of the smaller volute, unlike the larger one, are not dictated by the

overall length and projection of the bracket, and can be adjusted to accommodate the need for a smooth transition. In our example this reversing curve has the same radius each way, using the centers of the eyes as the axis; the centers and radii of the two arcs are shown on the side elevation in Fig 4.24. The fillet meets the wall of the smaller circle, which frames a simple flower. To add interest to the broad, flat fillet, a flute is run down its center. By the same token, the triangular space between volute and terminating circle is relieved by a flat-bottomed recess to create more depth.

## PREPARING THE BLANK

If glue-up is necessary to obtain the proper-sized block, the glue lines should be symmetrical when viewed from the front elevation. Ideally, the grain should be bookmatched so that visually it will remain symmetrical in the front view. Mark the front elevation centerline, and carry it around the back of the block as well, because bandsawing will remove the guidelines on the face. It may be helpful to mark the centerlines of the large volute on both sides, to help ensure that the two sides of the bracket match. This is a wise precaution even if using photocopied patterns. It is helpful to compare all the blanks by lining them up along a fence or straightedge or placing them back to back so that the eye can detect areas of dissimilarity.

Secure the pattern to the blank with masking tape along one edge only. Using the tape like a hinge, lift the pattern to make sure the alignment is correct and the large volute fits on the blank. Using two sheets of carbon paper back to back, you can trace the drawing onto one side of the blank and at the same time

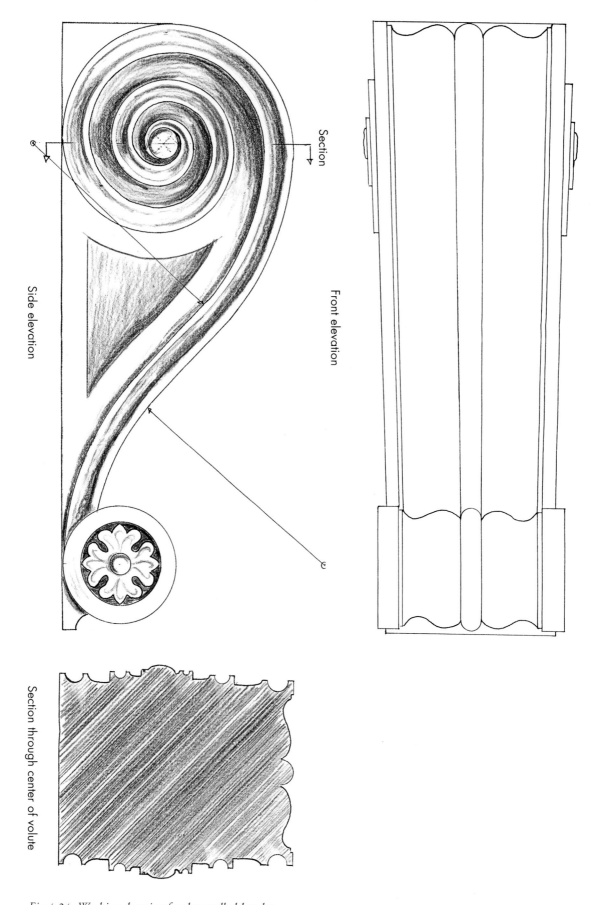

Section

Front elevation

Side elevation

Section through center of volute

Fig 4.24 *Working drawing for the scrolled bracket*

transfer the drawing to the reverse side of the pattern, creating a mirror-image pattern for use on the other side of the bracket. Mark all the same sides when doing multiple brackets, then flip them over to do the second sides.

After transferring the pattern, bandsaw the blank, checking that the blade is cutting perpendicular to the table. It is disheartening to cut the top side perfectly, only to find the bottom side has been shaved off. If there is any doubt, saw proud of the line and then plane or file until the sides match.

## CARVING THE VOLUTE

Noting where the recessed cove will be (you may prefer to shade it in pencil to avoid confusion), use a quick-sweep gouge (#9 or #11) to waste just outside the defining spiral line (Fig 4.25). This immediately shows where the recess will be, but also allows (as in any relief work) for subsequent setting in to the marked line. The gouge used for setting in will break away the wood between the marked line and the groove made by the quick gouge. Stabbing directly around the spiral without this preliminary groove would put strain on the surface wood and cause chip-out. Remember that the grain direction at the cutting edge of the gouge changes as the gouge describes a circle; a quarter-circle can be cut before a change of direction (and a change of hands) is necessary. The trickiest area is parallel to the grain, where the tool has a tendency to follow the grain, making the arc appear flat.

The next stage is to set in to the marked line using gouges of appropriate radii. Because gouges are made so that each sweep describes a circle when rotated vertically, each width of a particular sweep describes a different concentric circle. Spirals have arcs with decreasing radii, so a sequence of sweeps is necessary to define them. Use shallower gouges for the outer arc (Fig 4.26), increasing in quickness as you work inward. In trying to match the available tools to a particular arc, it is best to err on the shallow side (Fig 4.27), because facets which may be left by a shallow gouge can be smoothed out easily enough, whereas divots caused by the wings of a gouge too quick are nearly impossible to remove. Of course, matching gouge to curve may be limited by the tools in one's collection. Begin with the outside line (already partially defined by the bandsawn edge), with the bevel of the gouge toward the waste side, and stab vertically. There is no need to cut deeply at this stage: if using a mallet, a few taps will do for now. Proceed by keeping the blade of the tool in its

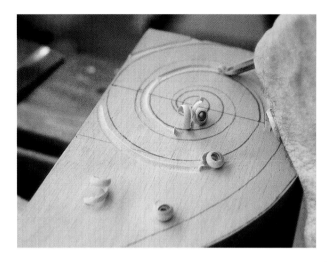

*Fig 4.25 Carving sequence: relieving around the line of the spiral in preparation for setting in*

*Fig 4.26 Beginning to set in around the spiral with a shallow gouge*

*Fig 4.27 Setting in toward the center of the volute. If a gouge of the exact radius is not available, choose a shallower rather than a deeper one*

own cut and sliding it toward uncut wood, then stabbing again. Continue setting in by this self-tracking method until the shallow gouge ceases to follow the spiral line; then select a smaller gouge of the same sweep, or a slightly quicker one of similar size. See that it matches the last cut of the previous gouge before proceeding. You will have to change gouges several times to complete the spiral. A combination of sweeps #5, #6, and #7 will usually be sufficient on all but extreme sizes of volutes.

Set in carefully around the eye. More often than not the eye projects beyond the fillet, which slopes away from it. Often, to save time and material, a hemispherical "button" is glued on to form the eye, but our example is made in one piece. Under these circumstances it is best to round over the eye at this stage, so that it is less likely to be split off while carving the rest of the bracket. This also serves as a starting point from which to slope the fillet.

Clean up the area between the vertical defining cuts of the volute. This should be a simple matter. Because the volute will spiral from the eye downward, cleaning up this area begins to form an incline (Fig 4.28). Repeated setting in will be required as this process continues. Work the incline on a shallow angle from the eye outward, so that the eye is left protruding slightly. Ideally, a flat chisel (#1) would produce the flattest surface, but using a #2 or #3 gouge avoids the scratches and divots which the corners of the chisel are liable to cause. When the incline has been worked all around the volute, sight from an oblique angle to see if the incline is even, without dips, and flat. Viewed in

Fig 4.28 Beginning to form the inclined surface of the volute

this way the succeeding revolutions should appear parallel (Fig 4.29).

Using the finger-fence method of marking, redraw the line defining the arris or corner between fillet and cove (Fig 4.30). With a #7 gouge, pivot around this inner line to begin carving the cove, in the same manner as in the original wasting. After working this cove around, shaving close to the line, repeat using a #8 or #9 gouge right up to the arris. This makes for a nearly 90° corner at the surface while maintaining the curved bottom of the cove. Again, several different-sized tools are necessary to work the cove all around. Near the eye it is difficult to work the tool along the spiral, so stabbing from the side should be used instead

Fig 4.29 The incline completed: a view from the side should show a continuous gentle slope from center to edge

(Fig 4.31)—the cove is so small here that this change of technique is not noticeable. Fig 4.32 shows this stage completed. As will be obvious, sloping the fillet back from the eye of the large volute reduces the width of the bracket at the end where the small volute is. It is imperative for the two sides of the bracket to be even, so measure and mark the new width using the center-line on the back of the bracket (carried anew to the front). As the cove opens into the triangular space between the volute and the rear edge of the bracket, the ground should be sunk as far as the smaller circle at the opposite end. To break up this flat expanse, a flat-bottomed recess is made which echoes the surrounding perimeter. The level of the small circle should also

be lowered, but it should remain above the fillet, as shown in the drawing of the front elevation. The method of carving the rosette inside the circle (Fig 4.33) will be explained in the following chapter. Finally, a flute is centered on the fillet to break up the flat surface (Fig 4.34).

At its simplest, the front elevation is left unmodeled, but usually a symmetrical profile is carved. This is often a combination of astragal and cyma curves, confined at the outer edges by fillets. There is no need to draw a pattern for this work, as several lines defining the center bead and the side fillets will suffice (Figs 4.35 and 4.36). Though the profile will diminish in width from the large volute to the smaller end, the border

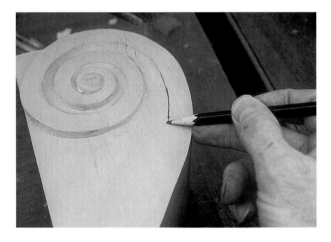

Fig 4.30  Marking the fillet around the volute and along the rest of the profile, using the tip of the middle finger as a fence to guide the pencil

Fig 4.32  The cavetto around the volute completed

Fig 4.31  Near the center of the volute, the cavetto is best cut from the side with a #7 gouge; the rest of the shaded section can be cut along the line of the spiral, using first a #7 and then a deeper gouge

Fig 4.33  The rosette in the small circle

Fig 4.34  *The flute running down the center of the fillet is an optional refinement in this design*

Fig 4.35  *Marking the front fillets with a pencil gauge*

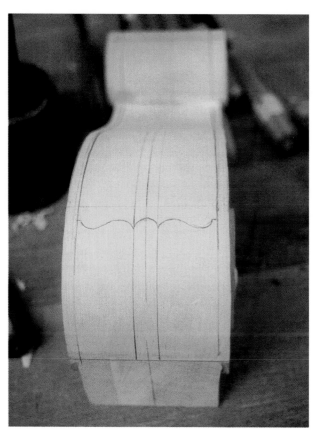

Fig 4.36  *The fillets marked out, with a schematic section of the center bead and flanking cyma profiles*

Fig 4.37  *Rounding over the convex part of the cyma with an inverted gouge. A backbent gouge is helpful where the curve changes direction near the lower baluster. Some filing and sanding will be needed to produce a uniform finish*

fillets are kept the same width throughout, making the bead and cyma do the reducing. This profile usually circles the baluster or roll as well.

Fig 4.37 shows carving in progress. A parting tool can be used to separate the astragal from the flanking cyma profiles. The bead can then be rounded over using a medium gouge turned over; using a semicircular #9 for this is difficult, as the wings of the gouge dig into the valley created by the parting tool. As the curve begins to flatten and butt against the baluster, a backbent #7 will allow the correct angle to work the profiles. Often there is a flat plane at the bottom of the valley, in which case there is more room for quicker gouges. The concave part of the cyma is worked next. The convex part can again be rounded with the gouge turned over. The curve of transition between the two elements of the cyma is broader than the curve meeting the bead, so a flatter gouge or backbent gouge can be used here.

A reasonably nice surface can be obtained with gouges, but files and sandpaper on rigid forms (laths, dowels, V-blocks) will be necessary to get sufficient smoothness for truly clean, crisp shapes. The challenge is to work the tool marks into a smooth surface which requires the minimum amount of sanding. Though irregularity in some types of carving is permissible—indeed charming—in such a strict geometric form as the volute unevenness is immediately discernible and distracting, especially in a capital or **cartouche** where volutes are placed adjacent to each other. Among some carvers the notion of sanding may send chills down the spine, but in architectural work it is often necessary. Files should be used for shaping and smoothing as much as possible, but they are limited in their ability to turn interior corners. There are many gadgets and gizmos on the market to take the drudgery out of sanding, but simple shop-made blocks are as good as anything, because one can constantly customize them. Dowels, stock with rounded edges, and foam paint rollers can be used for concavities. Blocks with various angles on their edges and even old credit cards can be used for the tight spots. Most sanding, however, is done with the tips of the fingers. Mechanical sanders, even the recently introduced profile sanders, are not very sensitive to the material, much less the decoration. Flap wheels, as used in industry, tend to round over the crisp edges of the carving and should not be used

except very lightly to clean up fuzz. A judicious use of the finer grits is all that should be needed, and sanding should only be used after all the carving has been accomplished.

Figs 4.38 and 4.39 show the completed bracket.

## VARIATIONS

A common treatment, as we saw before, is an acanthus leaf undulating down the front of the bracket and curling up at the lower baluster. A plain tongue-like leaf can also be used, as in Fig 4.18. The acanthus is often in fairly high relief and so lifelike as to defy the bordering fillets by overlapping them. The lower roll in this case can either have the previously described astragal and cyma configuration or, in keeping with the foliage theme, leaves sprouting from the center bead and oriented to the length of the baluster. Fig 6.7 shows this latter treatment on the baluster of an Ionic capital.

Another use of the volute in combination with other elements is taken up in Chapter 6, where carving the Ionic capital is explained.

Fig 4.38 The completed bracket from the side

Fig 4.39 A three-quarter view of the completed bracket, showing the bead and cyma treatment on the front

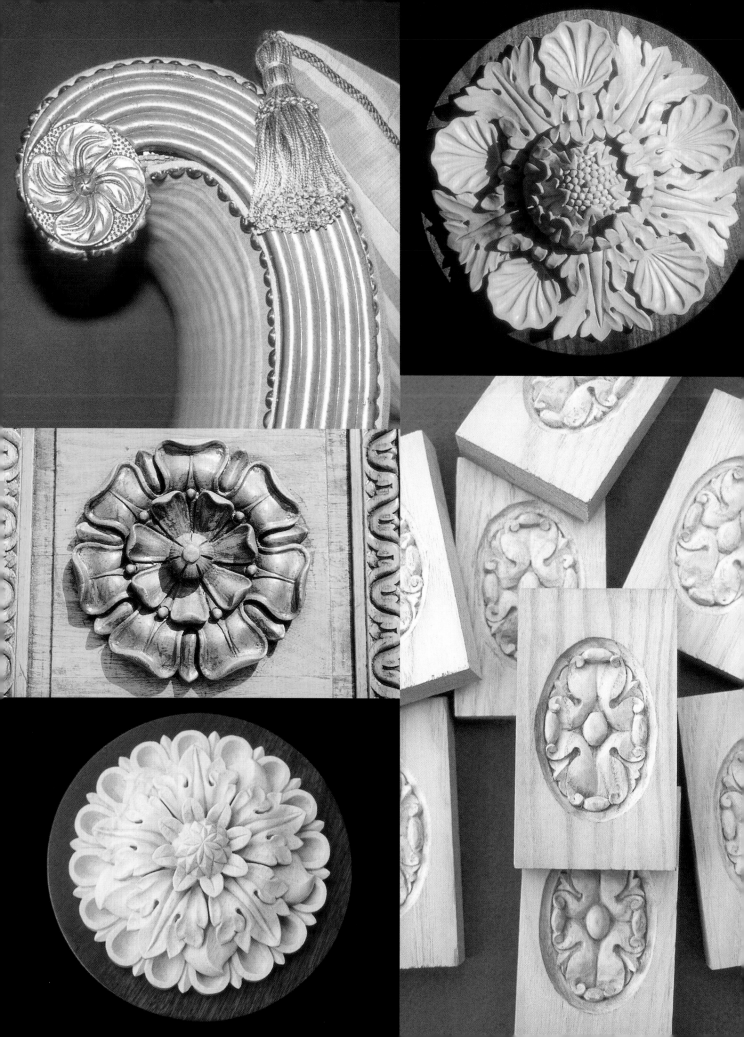

# ROSETTES

## Incised • Applied • High relief

**R**osette is a general term for a round or ovoid depiction of a flower (Figs 5.1 and 5.2). A few geometrically abstract chip-carved incisions may be called rosettes, but usually rosettes are recognizably flowers, with a central disk and petals, with or without leaves radiating outward. Some rosettes are highly modeled and undercut, and may have other objects from nature, such as shells and birds, among the foliage (Fig 5.3). *Paterae* (**patera**, singular) are circular, relatively small, evenly spaced decorations on frieze or architrave, often in the form of a plain disk or a simple flower (Fig 5.4).

> *Gibbons's assistants were fortunate to have a master to advise and correct them; but at heart, like all knowledge and every skill, woodcarving is self-taught.*
>
> DAVID ESTERLY

Rosettes are found in many situations where a square or rectangular space is defined by surrounding elements. They are found in the metopes of the Doric frieze (Figs 5.5 and 5.6), in coffers of a vault or ceiling, and in door panels (Figs 5.7 and 5.8). They often occur in the square space created by the intersection of flat moldings, as on **crossetted** picture frames, overmantels (Fig 5.9; see also Fig 7.6), and door architraves. They sometimes form an element within another design, such as the guilloche or the volute (Fig 5.10; see also Figs 2.21, 4.11, 4.18, 4.21). They are sometimes also found on the necking of the Roman Doric order.

*Fig 5.1 Circular rosette of low-relief foliage*

*Fig 5.2  A set of plaques with incised oval rosettes*

*Fig 5.4  A painted rosette or patera typical of those found on Greek temples*

*Fig 5.3  A more elaborate high-relief rosette with shells between the leaves*

*Fig 5.5  Rosettes between triglyphs on a Doric frieze, echoed by smaller ones in the soffit above; Drayton Hall, Charleston, SC (Drayton Hall, a National Trust Historic Site/Frederick Wilbur)*

Fig 5.6  Doric frieze with applied rosettes between triglyphs; detail of the desk and bookcase shown in Fig 1.11 (collection of Mr and Mrs George M. Kaufman)

Fig 5.7  Applied rosette on door panel, Washington, DC

Fig 5.8  Whorled leaf rosette on a panel in the Hammond–Harwood House, Annapolis, MD (Hammond–Harwood House Association/Frederick Wilbur)

Fig 5.9  Whorled leaf rosette on overmantel (by courtesy of Mrs James C. Wheat/photograph Frederick Wilbur)

Fig 5.10 *A console bracket in which a rosette replaces the customary volute*

On furniture, rosettes can be found on plinths, pilaster blocks, and the square parts of turned table legs; they are also used, as Figs 5.11 and 5.12 show, to terminate scrolled sofa arms and scrolled pediments.

In keeping with its decorative function, the floral forms used in the rosette are invariably stylized rather than naturalistic. Fig 5.13, for example, shows the real-life flowers of dogwood (*Cornus florida*). In Fig 5.14 the flower has been stylized, especially with respect to the regularization of the leaves at the corners. (The flowers actually bloom before the leaves appear.) The same flower is shown as an **applied** rosette in Fig 5.15. There are, of course, some flowers which do not lend themselves to being depicted as rosettes because they are too complex, or not easily made symmetrical.

Fig 5.11 *Rosette on sofa arm, 1815–25 (Colonial Williamsburg Foundation/Frederick Wilbur)*

Fig 5.13 *Dogwood flowers*

Fig 5.12 *Rosette on scrolled pediment of reproduction eighteenth-century highboy (by courtesy of Mrs Robert L. Wilbur)*

There are several similar ornaments which may be confused with the rosette. The **sunburst** is of round or oval shape and consists of radiating reeds. The **fan**, so popular in the eighteenth century, is similar to the sunburst, and usually has flutes set in triangular or semicircular shapes resembling a scallop shell. **Medallions** are plaques of any shape which depict in relief an isolated object such as a human head, figures, or manmade objects.

## THE INCISED ROSETTE

The first stage in laying out the incised rosette is to divide the circle into the required number of sectors; extend the division lines beyond the circle so that they can easily be redrawn if necessary after carving has begun.

Define the outer circle with a parting tool and use a gouge of the appropriate radius to set in the center circle, the disk of the blossom. The example shown has a dished ground; alternatively, the outer circle could be set in perpendicularly to the surface (or routed) to gain more depth. The parting tool *can* be used to define the petal divisions, but setting in with vertical cuts gives clearer definition (Fig 5.16). At the outside edge, care should be taken not to stab too deeply. Stab in the ends of the petals.

Fishtail gouges are useful to take the ground (such as it is) down around the petals. Care should be taken to leave no ridge between the original parting tool circle and the finished ground (Fig 5.17). If you do not

Fig 5.15 *Stylized dogwood flower for use as an applied rosette*

Fig 5.16 Carving sequence: *setting in the incised rosette*

Fig 5.14 *Stylized dogwood flower used in an incised rosette*

Fig 5.17 *Grounding between the petals with a fishtailed flat gouge*

Fig 5.18 *Cleaning the ground between the petals with a narrow grounding tool; a ground-down nail is an acceptable substitute*

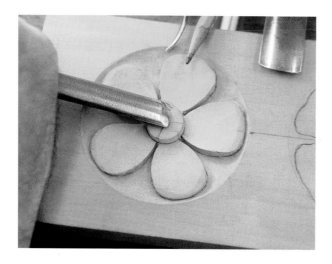

Fig 5.19 *Rounding the central disk with an inverted gouge*

have a sufficiently narrow grounding tool (Fig 5.18), a small cut nail, ground to the appropriate width, can be used to clear the narrow space between the petals. It may be necessary to set in again at this point: the ground should be sufficiently deeper than the petals to make the flower appear to float on the dark shadows behind it.

Fig 5.21 *Three variations on the simple incised flower; the right-hand example boasts a second layer of petals*

Fig 5.22 *A further variation on the incised rosette*

Fig 5.20 *The incised rosette completed*

Slope the petals toward the center disk and round over the disk (Fig 5.19). The edges of the petals should be slightly beveled and the petals veined at the center; Fig 5.20 shows the final result.

Undercutting is not necessary. Though the petals can have more swagger or character if desired, naturalism is not the primary goal here. Figs 5.21 and 5.22 show a few of the possible variations.

## APPLIED ROSETTES

In many uses the rosette is carved independently from the structural members of the piece and subsequently applied to the surface, as in Figs 5.5, 5.7, and 5.9.

The two rosettes described in the following sequence illustrate how the round design can be stretched to fill a square space (the width of the latter being the same as the diameter of the former). Fig 5.23 shows the two designs marked out on the wood before being bandsawn to shape. To hold the sawn blank, a recess is routed into waste stock and several small brads are driven into it; the heads are snipped off and the blank is pressed onto them.

Carving begins with establishing the sectional profile (Fig 5.24). The hemispherical or domed central disk is shaped first. From this, the leaves spring up and then flow to the background in a cyma or reversing curve. Sometimes, as in a Tudor rose, petals or leaves, especially when confined by a bordering circle, may curl back toward the center of the rosette (see Figs 5.7–5.9, and Fig 7.14).

The eyes are drilled next, to establish the divisions between the leaves. The leaves are set in—that is, shaped in silhouette—and the secondary leaf tips are relieved in order to define the main leaf (Fig 5.25). The smaller, overlapping leaflets are set in, then the veins and the surface modeling complete the design.

*Fig 5.23  Carving sequence for applied rosettes: designs traced on board*

*Fig 5.25  The leaves are set in and the tips of the under leaves lowered*

*Fig 5.24  The shapes have been cut out on the bandsaw or scrollsaw and are held in routed recesses on waste board. The cross-sectional shape is defined first, beginning with the central dome*

Finally, a slight undercutting of the bottom leaves brings the whole rosette off the surface background. This can be quickly done with a knife after extricating the rosette from its holding board. To further enhance the appearance of depth, the rosette is sometimes let into a recess (Figs 5.26 and 5.27). Fig 5.28 shows a more elaborate variation in which the recess, edged with a cavetto molding, creates strong shadows to show off the delicate undercutting.

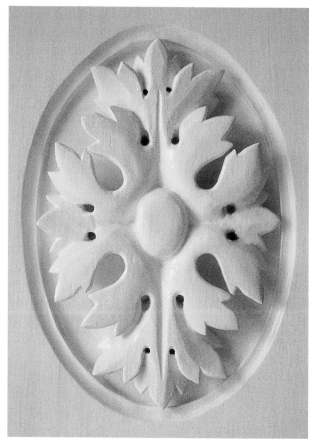

Fig 5.28 A strongly undercut rosette within an oval recess (see Figs 7.24 and 7.33d)

Fig 5.26 The square rosette completed and set into its recess; undercutting of the leaf tips is clearly visible

To produce small disks for 2in (50mm) or smaller rosettes, a hole saw mounted in a drill press and without its centering drill can be used. Use stock which is a little thicker than the depth of the saw blade, so that the disks don't jam in the saw. The stock must be firmly secured to the drill press table. The disks can be popped out or quickly sawn out on a bandsaw.

## A HIGH-RELIEF ROSETTE

Inspired by Renaissance and baroque examples, this rosette makes use of three turned and carved layers. The intention is to create a deeply sculpted piece. In designing this type of rosette, the front elevation and the section must be considered simultaneously. Fig 5.29 shows the layered sequence, with the sections of each layer. Using a series of tracings one can build up the design, just as computer drawing programs do. This not only allows rotation and adjustment of the design to exploit the method to maximum advantage, but also separates the elements literally into layers. It should be a logical step from here to create the

Fig 5.27 The round rosette set in its recess

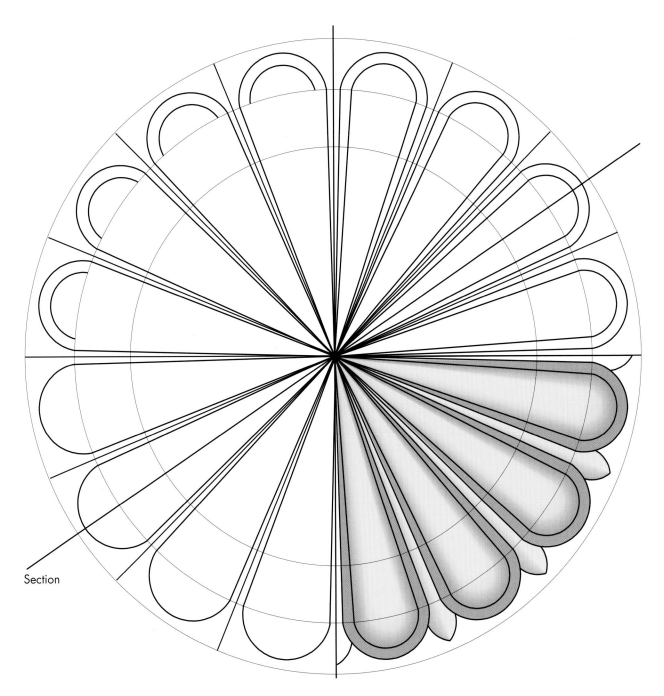

Section

*Fig 5.29 Working drawings for the high-relief rosette, showing layers and sections (adapted with permission from* Woodwork *Magazine #54, December 1998)*
(a) *Plan of the first (lowest) layer*

section drawing, using several pieces of tracing paper. Unless there is some separation between the layers, there is not much point in using this method; there must be some "see-through" from one layer to the next. A large plate-glass window can be used as a light box. By taping successive layers of tracing paper to the glass, each drawn element can be shifted quickly to the next division line.

In this example, the bottom layer is a shell-like or fluted geometric pattern with strong lines, and is deeply cut. This layer has an even number of divisions and acts as a background for the naturalistic foliage on top of it. The middle layer is sandwiched onto the bottom layer and provides the visual bulk of the design: it has a flowing curve to its section and shows the most complexity in its elements. As an alternative to the leaves

(b) *Plan of the second layer*

(c) *Plan of the third layer*

overlapping each other, more "see-through" could have been designed. In fact, this layer could have been hollowed out on the back as well. An odd number of main elements for the middle layer seems more visually interesting than an even number, which when matched up with the regular layer beneath would tend to give a static appearance.

The topmost layer is nested into the middle layer so that the petals pop out of the foliage. Reverting to simple shapes and an even number of petals, it seems to stabilize the profusion of detail in the middle foliage, and the composition appears balanced and under control. The regular pyramidal divisions of the flower disk reinforce the geometry of the first layer.

Turning the pieces is uncomplicated, except for nesting the last piece into the middle layer; enough

Section

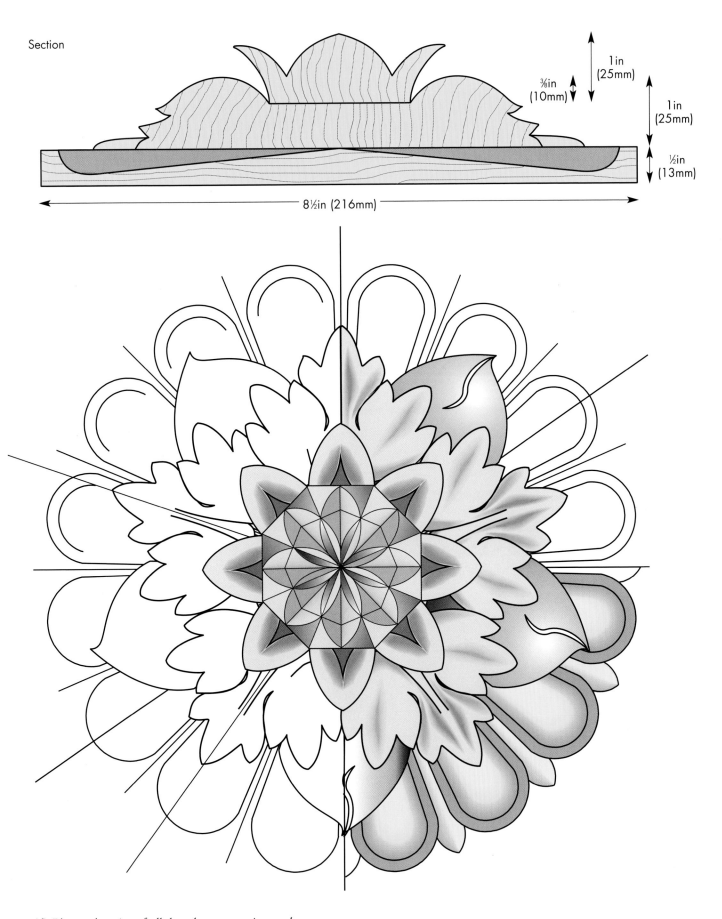

1in
(25mm)

⅜in
(10mm)

1in
(25mm)

½in
(13mm)

8½in (216mm)

(d) *Plan and section of all three layers superimposed*

clearance is necessary to give the desired effect, but not so much as to make the join obvious. The first layer doesn't really need to be turned, but accuracy is easier to achieve on the lathe. The middle layer has a cyma profile, the same as the rosettes described earlier, which is shaped by eye (Fig 5.30). The center is recessed to accommodate the last layer. If a screw chuck is used to turn the last layer, the piece can be removed for fitting and remounted for further refinement as necessary.

To lay out the various pieces, a framing square is placed on the lathe bed and aligned with the center point. The center can be obtained easily as the blank is spinning on the lathe. The various divisions are then easily marked by means of the indexing head on the lathe, or a protractor. The grain of all three layers should be oriented in the same direction, to disguise the layering as well as to coordinate shrinkage. The first layer is easy to lay out on the bench (Fig 5.31). For the profiled middle layer it is easier to start the layout on the back and carry the lines around the edges. To translate the flat design to a curved profile some adjustment is required. A piece of tracing paper laid flat on the profile, marked, and then placed over

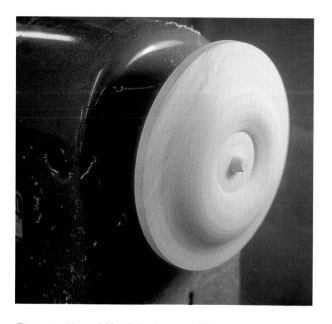

Fig 5.30 Turned blank for the second layer

Fig 5.32 The second layer with the upper leaves marked out; note how the design worked out on the flat drawing needs to be stretched to fit the convex surface

Fig 5.31 The first layer laid out

*Fig 5.33 The second layer fully marked out, ready for fitting the last layer into the center*

the original drawing will make stretching the design easier (Figs 5.32 and 5.33). The small third layer can be drawn by eye.

Bandsaw or scrollsaw the outlines of the two bottom layers and clean up with file, gouge, or knife. The bottom layer can easily be held to the bench with C-clamps (G-cramps). The profiled second layer is held with a carver's screw made from a large hanger bolt with appropriate washers, inserted through a dog hole in the bench. One advantage of this method is that the piece can easily be rotated as one works around the form.

## CARVING THE LAYERS

The main challenge in carving this rosette is the constantly changing grain. For the first layer, begin with a parting tool to define the separation between flutes, creating in the process the ridges of the short peaks which poke out between them. Use various sizes of deep gouge to dig out the trough, changing direction as the grain demands; at the rounded end use a #8 to scoop out the depth (Fig 5.34). Ideally the flute should be either semicircular or U-shaped in depth, becoming shallower as it narrows toward the center (Fig 5.35). It makes little sense to spend time on the area which will

*Fig 5.34 Carving the first layer: the segments are defined with the parting tool and the flutes carved with a range of deep gouges, blending the cuts as smoothly as possible*

*Fig 5.35 The first layer completed and ready for sanding. The central area need not be carefully finished*

be covered by the second layer. Make use of the corners or "wings" of the gouges to smooth the transitions between the different sizes of gouge. After a light sanding of the flutes, sand the flat face in order to crisp up the arrises between them.

The middle layer is treated in the same way as the small rosette described above; begin by setting in and then paring down the lower leaves, which in turn are modeled and undercut. The central vein should extend all the way into the recess made for the third layer—you can be sure that someone is going to peek under the petals! Fig 5.36 shows the use of a hacksaw blade to clear the narrow channels between the leaves.

A drinking straw is useful for blowing the chips out of the deep eyes.

The petals of the third layer may be shaped with a knife or a gouge. Figs 5.37 and 5.38 give two views of this last layer before carving, and Fig 5.39 shows it after the petals have been shaped by gouge and/or knife. The parting tool defines the cross-hatching of the flower disk, but a flat chisel is used to create the actual pyramids. Assemble the layers with glue, and screw them together through pilot holes from the back. Mount the finished rosette on a background of contrasting-colored wood in order to protect the carving and set it off from its surroundings (Fig 5.40).

*Fig 5.36 Second layer: using a hacksaw blade to clean the small spaces between leaves*

*Fig 5.37 Side view showing the uncarved third layer nestled into the completed second layer*

*Fig 5.38 Plan view at the same stage, showing the third layer laid out by eye*

*Fig 5.39 The completed high-relief rosette, fully assembled*

*Fig 5.40 The rosette mounted on a contrasting walnut backing*

CHAPTER

# CAPITALS

Stiff leaf • Ionic • Romanesque • Tower of the Winds • Corinthian

Capitals have the structural function of enlarging the bearing surface of a vertical column, thereby adding support to the beams (architraves) and the roof. The Doric capital, though it has some geometric decoration, looks like a simple cushion, the **echinus**, supporting a flat plate, the **abacus**. Of the three Greek orders, two require carved capitals: the Ionic and the Corinthian. But to avoid oversimplifying, it must be pointed out that there has been an evolution in the forms and that there are numerous variations and combinations. For example, the Tower of the Winds (48 BCE) at Athens, illustrated later in this chapter, combines the stiff or palm leaf with the acanthus. The Romans combined the Corinthian and the Ionic to make the Composite order, and also created the Tuscan, probably derived from Etruscan antecedents. The Renaissance and baroque embellished these capitals almost beyond recognition (see Fig 6.76).

A simple capital or echinus can be made from a series of moldings that stand out progressively further as they ascend to support the abacus or architrave. The combined ovolo and astragal, as on the Ionic capital, ostensibly fulfill this function. Often these moldings are carved with egg and dart or with gadrooning (Fig 6.1; see also Fig 2.1), in association with the bead and billet astragal. Often a necking below these moldings is fluted or carved with anthemion. The capital from the Erechtheion (see Fig 6.10) shows this well.

## THE STIFF-LEAF CAPITAL

This capital may derive from the papyrus capital of Egypt, though it no doubt has multiple origins. Because of its relative ease in fabrication, this capital is common on many pieces of furniture: pilasters on highboys, bedposts, and even harps and other musical instruments. Fig 6.2 shows a mirror frame, of which the top section probably contained a scene or other decoration in *verre églomisé*—a technique which involves painting on the reverse side of the glass.

The bell-shaped or flaring blank for the stiff-leaf capital can be completely turned, and then carved while still mounted on the lathe. A lathe with an indexing head is helpful for laying out the units, but "walking" around the turning with a pair of dividers can be just as easy. The tool-rest positioned near the turning can act as a marking fence, if set parallel to the turning axis. The flared section that will be carved usually has a bead at its smaller end to separate the capital from the shaft of the column. This makes it a congé molding in the round. There is usually an outer ring of leaves that overlaps a second layer.

As with any foliage molding, all the leaves are stabbed in and the ground between the leaf ends sunk to the desired level. The leaves of the second layer are then lowered sufficiently to define the primary layer. The primary leaves are separated by a parting tool or a narrow grounding tool. These outer leaves are then modeled and detailed. The stiff leaf proper has a middle vein and edges that are at surface level, with a pair of flutes separating them. The tips of the second layer are not often modeled. The *sinuated* (waved) leaf has a series of undulations along its margins, which may curl over slightly (Figs 6.3 and 6.4). The bell-shaped turning can be made with extra flare and additional material at the top to allow for a slightly curled leaf.

> *Let no one ignorant of geometry enter my doors.*
>
> SAID TO HAVE BEEN INSCRIBED OVER THE DOOR OF PLATO'S ACADEMY

Fig 6.1  Ovolo molding used as capital on pilaster,
University of Virginia (note acroterion on pediment above)

Fig 6.2  Stiff-leaf capital on a mirror frame (by courtesy of
Thomas A. Goddard)

Fig 6.3  A set of stiff-leaf
pilaster capitals

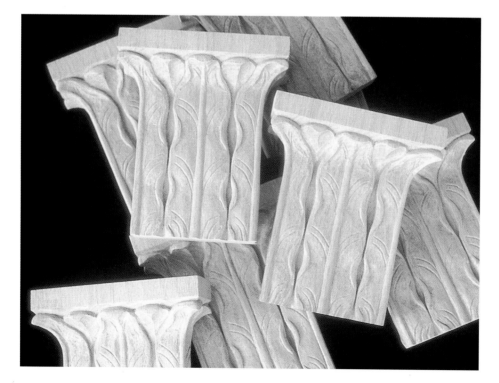

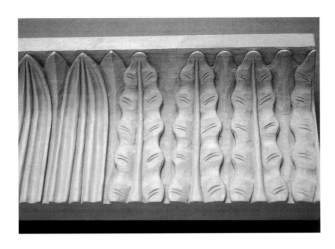

*Fig 6.4 Two kinds of stiff leaf; that on the right is said to be* sinuated

This type of capital can be used in a number of furniture situations to retain the slender quality of a column or group of columns. Fig 6.5 shows a stiff-leaf pilaster capital with the addition of volutes.

## THE IONIC CAPITAL

In the Western tradition, the voluted capital derives from the Egyptian lotus as depicted in various ancient wall paintings. It first appears in Aegean art as two opposing spirals, like a letter V with curly serifs, between which a palmette or blossom sprouts; this form is known as the Aeolic capital. Though there

have been numerous experiments with the form through the millennia, the basic proportions as set down by Vitruvius, Palladio, and others are still considered appropriate. The capital is half a module high overall—that is, half the diameter of the column at its base. The eyes of the volutes are one diameter apart and, because the shaft tapers toward the top of the column, the volutes project on either side. Fig 6.6, from an eighteenth-century edition of Palladio, shows the capital in elevation and reflected plan, together with an elevation of the base; it also shows the same method of drawing the volute which was used in Chapter 4.

The capital in its classic form consists of two opposing volutes draped over a circling egg and dart molding (the echinus), surmounted by a square abacus. The front and back of the capital are the same, and these faces are connected along the sides by a roll known as a **baluster** or bolster (Figs 6.7 and 6.8). This difference in orientation presents a problem at the corners of a building, which is usually solved by setting two voluted faces on adjacent sides, with the two back-to-back volutes projecting at 45° from the capital, while the two inner sides have balusters. The photograph of the temple of Athena Nike (see Fig 1.4) shows this very clearly. In some instances, all four sides have voluted faces. Later, the Italian Vincenzo Scamozzi (1552–1616) is credited with having used and popularized this variant, so it is now called a Scamozzi capital (Fig 6.9).

*Fig 6.5 A stiff-leaf capital with volutes*

**105**

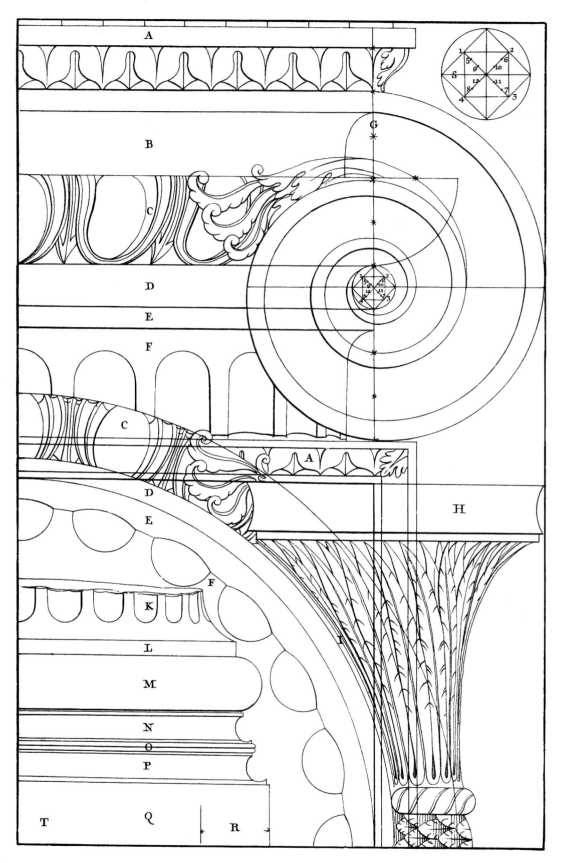

Fig 6.6  Details of the Ionic order, from Isaac Ware's 1738 edition of Palladio: elevation and reflected plan of capital, with (bottom left) partial elevation of column base and (top right) detail of the method of drawing the volute (by courtesy of Dover Publications, Inc.)

Fig 6.7 Ionic capital with stiff-leaf baluster, Charleston, SC

The primary difference between the Greek and Roman versions is that the former has larger volutes, and the connection between the two curves downward, while the Roman is tighter, and has a straight cavetto connection. Compare Fig 6.10, the capital from the Erechtheion, with Fig 6.11, a typical Roman capital. As the capital of All Souls' Church, Langham Place, London shows (Fig 6.12), even angels bless the Ionic capital! Palladio shows an example in which the cavetto of the volute is infilled with foliage, as in Fig 6.13. Figs 6.14 and 6.15 show the Ionic capital used in pilaster form, in a corner cupboard and a ceremonial chair back.

Fig 6.8 Beaded astragals on the baluster of a Greek-style capital, University of Virginia

Fig 6.10 Greek Ionic capital from the Erechtheion, British Museum (British Museum/Frederick Wilbur)

Fig 6.9 A Scamozzi capital, with volutes on each side, at the Hammond–Harwood House, Annapolis, MD (Hammond–Harwood House Association/Frederick Wilbur)

Fig 6.11 The Roman version of the Ionic capital

Fig 6.12 Angel replaces flower on a Scamozzi-type capital, All Souls' Church, Langham Place, London

Fig 6.13 Ionic capital with foliage, after Palladio

Fig 6.14 Ionic pilaster on a corner cupboard, 1790–1800 (Colonial Williamsburg Foundation/Frederick Wilbur)

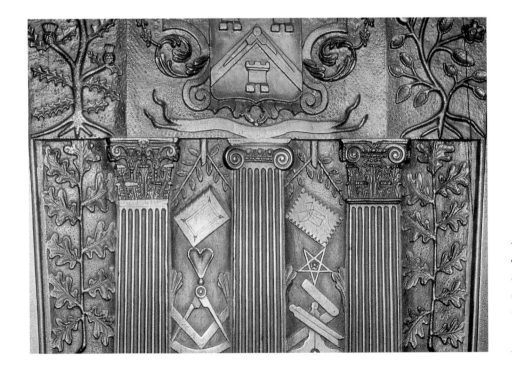

Fig 6.15 Corinthian, Ionic, and Composite capitals incorporated into a ceremonial chair back, c.1765 (Colonial Williamsburg Foundation/ Frederick Wilbur)

## PREPARING THE BLANK

The blank for the Ionic capital is a little more difficult to fabricate than that for the stiff leaf, as the volutes drop below the joint between capital and column, so no portion of the profile can be turned on the lathe. There are three horizontal divisions to the capital. The moldings which circle the column are always an astragal surmounted by an ovolo, and are usually carved with bead and billet and egg and dart, respectively. In some cases the astragal circles the column beneath the baluster. The ovolo is "covered" by the volutes draped over it, not unlike a scrolled piece of parchment laid there by an absent-minded philosopher! The abacus is molded with a cyma reversa, which is often carved with the waterleaf.

In Chapter 4 we discussed the drawing of the volute, and the same method can be used here. (The pattern seen in Fig 6.19 is a tracing from the original drawing, with the arris between fillet and cove sketched in.) A front elevation, side elevation, and reflected plan should be drawn. The latter is a drawing showing the capital as if one had cut the column through and were looking up at the capital from below. This will aid in the preparation of the blank. The capital illustrated is of the Roman type, with a horizontal cavetto between volutes and sprouts of foliage overlapping the egg and dart.

The blank should be laid out with all centerlines, circles, and the face pattern of the volutes, before any machine work is begun. It is a good idea to describe the circle of the column on the bottom as well. The better to disguise the joint between column and capital, a recess the size of the former can be turned into the prepared blank (Figs 6.16 and 6.17). It is advisable to run the cyma molding above the volutes (which is the edge of the abacus) separately, and apply it to shoulders machined on the blank (visible in Figs 6.16 and 6.18). There are several reasons for this. First, carving the profile *in situ* would be time-consuming. Second, if it is to be carved with the usual waterleaf, the resulting end grain would be difficult. Third, the blank can easily be held in a vise by this protruding block for other operations. Fourth, while carving the end balusters the cyma will not be marred. Therefore the blank needs to be shaped to accommodate this addition.

Before turning the recess, some waste can be got out of the way. Using the table saw, make two cuts between the volutes to the depth of the underside of the capital (where the astragal begins). Clear the waste between the volutes with repeated passes through the

*Fig 6.16 Carving sequence: Ionic capital blanks seen from below (left) and above*

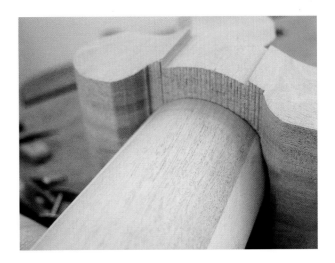

*Fig 6.17 The column fits into the turned recess in the underside of the capital*

*Fig 6.18 The volutes and the outline of the echinus have been bandsawn as far as possible*

*Fig 6.19  Re-marking the volutes from a cardboard template*

*Fig 6.20  The volute marked out and setting in begun*

*Fig 6.21  The volute is carved in the same way as that of the bracket in Chapter 4*

blade, or use a dado blade. While working on the table saw, the top of the blank should be shaped to accommodate the abacus with its cyma molding as mentioned previously. Do not be tempted to define the top of the protruding ovolo on the table saw, as the sprouts coming from the volutes are above this plane and would be cut off. The volutes can be bandsawn, allowing easier access for turning the bottom.

Obviously, care should be taken in turning the recess, especially if the columns have already been cut to length. In the event that the recess is too deep, shims can be used to correct the discrepancy. Mark the center of the recess, as this will locate the hole if a threaded rod is used to hold the base, column, and capital together; it is also used as the center for marking the outline of the astragal on the underside of the capital.

Next, bandsaw the remaining part of the outline of the volutes; remember to allow for the cyma molding at the top. The line of the volute should ease into the straight horizontal connection between volutes. It is wise to leave a slight flatness at the bottom so that the next operation can be performed without tilt, and so the bandsaw blade cuts perpendicular to the previously cut planes. Redraw the circular outline of the ovolo on the top shoulder, and draw the lines (visible on the right-hand capital in Fig 6.16) representing the front and back faces of the volutes. Bandsaw these faces, allowing spare material for the sprouts which spring from the volutes and overlap the egg and dart on the ovolo. Bandsaw as much as possible of the ovolo circle (Fig 6.18). This completes the machine work that can be done.

## CARVING

The basic shapes of the capital should be accurately formed with files before any carving begins. Later there will be shaping done by gouge as well. Start with the rolls, or balusters, at the ends of the capital, planing or filing to match the outer round of the volute. The volute must be laid out again, using a template traced from the drawing (Figs 6.19 and 6.20). For a series of identical capitals, it may be expedient to make a metal pattern in similar fashion to those used on moldings (see Chapter 2). One way of setting out the volute is to flatten the round area on the blank first, being careful not to intrude too far into the sprout. Alternatively, one can lay out over the bandsawn curve where the volute face slopes up to the sprout, as shown in the photographs; in this case, a slight tolerance for the

Fig 6.22 The flat ground
linking the two volutes
forms a "shelf" along the
top of the ovolo molding

curving plane may be necessary. Set in the spirals of the volutes and isolate the material that will become the sprouts (Fig 6.21).

Continue setting in and defining the fillets and coves of the volutes in a similar fashion to the voluted bracket described in Chapter 4. After both volutes have been cleaned up, the "shelf" or perpendicular plane which forms the top of the ovolo is defined with a flat chisel. Extend it as far as the material reserved for the sprouts as they curve from the top of the volute. The background—that is, the side face of the volute above the "shelf"—is brought down to the plane of the volute faces so as to connect with them in a continuous plane, parallel to the face of the capital (Fig 6.22). The coves of the volutes are then carried across above the ovolo so that these also connect, the fillet of the spiral flowing into the straight fillet at the top shoulder.

The last stage of the blocking out is to form the ovolo and the astragal (Figs 6.23 and 6.24). Mark the outline of the astragal on the underside, using a compass placed on the center mark in the bottom recess. With the blank in the vise, begin to pare down the lower section of these two convex moldings. Alternate between curving the ovolo down to the astragal and taking the astragal down toward the recess. Once you have excavated to the level of the astragal, the ovolo will be fully formed; the half-round of the astragal is then worked. With a parting tool, trench the inside corner between the astragal and the underside of the ovolo. Then, using a medium gouge turned over, begin rounding the astragal. A shallower gouge, also turned over, further refines the ovolo.

Fig 6.23 Shaping the ovolo with a shallow gouge, used bevel-side up

Fig 6.24 Preliminary shaping of the ovolo completed, leaving material for the sprouts at the beginning of the volute

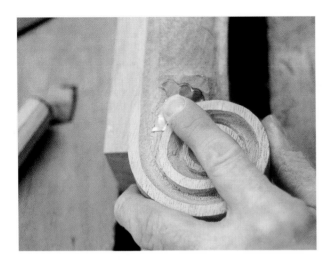

*Fig 6.25  Using a metal pattern to mark out the sprouts*

*Fig 6.26  The ends of the sprouts having been set in, the egg and dart is marked out next*

*Fig 6.27  The ovolo fully carved; only the astragal below it remains to be finished with bead and billet*

*Fig 6.28  Beginning to shape the baluster, with the capital clamped to the bench top*

A narrower gouge is necessary to reach the lower portion, under the material set aside for the sprouts. Remount the blank upside down in the vise so that the underside of the astragal can be rounded into the column recess; a backbent #7 is helpful in this. The astragal "disappears" into the baluster where it butts up against it (see Fig 6.26). You may have to mount the capital on its side once more to complete the rounding of the astragal. At this point the carving of the volutes and the blocking out of the remaining forms have been completed.

Next, lay out the egg and dart carving and the sprouts of foliage at the sides. Mark the limit of the sprouts using a pattern (Fig 6.25). An egg with its basket is centered on the ovolo between the volutes and, depending upon its size and proportions, a basket or a basket and a half can fit in before the molding meets the inside of the baluster, just behind the face of the volute (Fig 6.26). The sprouts springing from the top of the volute sweep down and cover the last egg. If a number of capitals are to be carved, secondary patterns for the sprout or for the entire ovolo might be helpful. Remember that the wood is mostly end grain in these corners, so slicing cuts work better than setting in with the mallet. Fig 6.27 shows this stage completed.

Carve the bead and billet next. The usual #9 gouge will be difficult to use on this small-diameter circle, where the grain changes quickly; instead, a little more fuss is necessary with a #7 gouge. In our example the bead is three-quarters round, and is seen more in silhouette against the column than in elevation as one

Fig 6.29 Using calipers to check the diameter of the baluster

would look up to it. On a larger, exterior capital, a fillet under the astragal would be added to set the capital off from the column (see Figs 6.8, 6.9, and 6.11).

The simple baluster illustrated here is carved with the capital first clamped to the bench top (Fig 6.28), then flipped over and held by the abacus block on the top. Calipers are used to ensure the two ends match (Fig 6.29). The completed capital, with the cyma molding in place on the abacus, is shown in Fig 6.30; Fig 6.31 shows it installed on the column.

The Ionic pilaster is worked similarly to the full round capital, except that the egg and dart molding is straight from volute to volute to echo the flat face of the pilaster shaft (Fig 6.32). Often the volutes flare outward (see Fig 2.3), as in the Scamozzi capital.

Fig 6.30 A set of Ionic capitals receiving their finishing touches; the cyma molding which represents the abacus is now in place

Fig 6.32 Ionic capitals for a pilaster

Fig 6.31 The finished capital mounted on its column

113

# A ROMANESQUE-STYLE CAPITAL

There are many varieties of capital which have leaves incorporated in them. The small pilaster capital in Fig 6.33 has a Romanesque feel; the volute gives it some grounding in classical tradition, but the leaves are varied in treatment.

Machine the blank slightly larger than the width and depth of the abacus, since the eyes as well as the extreme corners of the volutes project beyond it. Lay out the vertical centerline and carry it around the blank. Mark the outline of the abacus on the top, using a template or pattern (Fig 6.34). The bottom of the blank must match the dimensions of the pilaster. Using a pencil marking gauge, mark the extent of the volute and the fillet of the abacus. On some examples of this type of capital, the desired dimensions of abacus and pilaster may require that the corner leaf be skewed to some extent.

Begin by making stop cuts at the top of the volutes, then shape the abacus. A chisel with its beveled side down can be used as a plane to keep the fillet flat and square to the top (Fig 6.35). Then, with chisel or

Fig 6.33 A pilaster capital in the Romanesque idiom

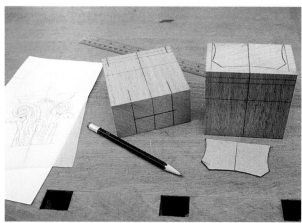

Fig 6.34 Using a template to mark the outline of the abacus on the top of the blank

Fig 6.35 Using a chisel to "plane" the concave face of the abacus

knife, define the volute by rounding the corners of the blank as in Figs 6.36 and 6.37. This creates a valley between volute and abacus. Check the round of the volute by looking at it from a 45° angle to the face of the blank.

The upper edge of the volute's fillet springs from the centerline and nearly touches the abacus fillet before blending into the rounded outside surface which has just been created. The outline then spirals in to form the eye. This is drawn freehand, though a few measurements can be taken to ensure symmetry (Fig 6.38). Looking directly at the corner, as before, will show any discrepancies.

Select the tool (probably a #7) which will smoothly continue the round along the lower valley and onto the face of the blank (Fig 6.39). Continue selecting tools to

*Fig 6.37 Frequently sight from the corner to check that front and sides correspond*

*Fig 6.36 Defining the extent of the volute by rounding the corner*

*Fig 6.38 The volutes are drawn freehand on the front and side faces*

*Fig 6.39 A #7 gouge is likely to be suitable for beginning the curve of the volute*

follow the line of the volute toward its eye, just as described in Chapter 4. Then relieve these stab cuts (Fig 6.40). The curve from the top of the volute to the centerline is somewhat gentler, so a #5 will probably be chosen (Fig 6.41).

Set in the tips of the uppermost leaves at the center, so that the cove of the abacus can be worked. The leaves which appear to curl under or behind the volute at the inside must be set in before the volute is sloped down from the eye toward the centerline (Fig 6.42). It may be helpful to sketch the lower center leaf onto the face and side of the block so that stop cuts for the leaf tip can be positioned accurately (Fig 6.43). This allows the volute stem to be lowered further, reinforcing the impression that the central leaf projects further than the flanking leaves which swirl up to the volute. One

Fig 6.42 The leaf tip curling "behind" the volute is set in so that the volute stem can be lowered

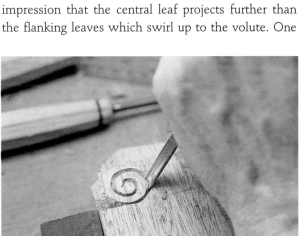

Fig 6.40 The spiral stab cuts are relieved

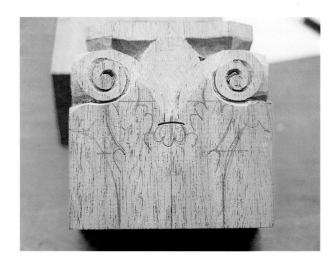

Fig 6.43 Sketching the leaves on the blank allows an accurate stop cut to be made for the tip of the middle leaf

Fig 6.41 A shallower gouge sets in the curve toward the centerline

Fig 6.44 The capital has now been tapered to the required pilaster dimensions and the center leaf isolated

Fig 6.45 *Using a try square to compare the positions of the center leaf tips from one capital to another*

will need to alternate between setting in and relieving as the volute stems are lowered.

The entire capital must now be sloped to the required dimensions at the bottom (Fig 6.44). The center leaf should have a gentle elliptical sweep from its projecting tip toward the base. The lower center leaf tip, however, projects above its surroundings. Because pilaster capitals are made in sets, or at least in pairs, a try square can be used to compare the leaf tips of each capital (Fig 6.45). The leaves are then redrawn freehand onto the face of the blank, and the separation between center, flanking, and corner leaves is made with the parting tool (Fig 6.46). The cove of the volute forms the ground for the adjoining leaf (Fig 6.47). In order to make the tip of this leaf appear to curl behind the volute, one should round the leaf over as in Fig 6.48.

Fig 6.46 *The main outlines of the leaves have been defined with the parting tool*

Fig 6.47 *Forming the cove of the volute also serves to outline the adjacent leaf*

Fig 6.48 *Rounding the leaf so that it appears to roll behind the volute*

This leaf should sweep toward the corner and then downward. The outlines of the leaves are stabbed in and relieved; Fig 6.49 shows the leaflets on the left stabbed in, while those on the right have been relieved. Care must be taken with the short grain of the leaf tips.

Continue differentiating the leaves until they are quite distinct. The leaf which curls below the volute is defined with a flat gouge; in relieving the adjacent leaf, the corner itself is created (Fig 6.50). The leaves between the volutes are separated. All the veins are then cut in, and the broad areas of the leaf surface sloped to meet them. Finally, a sweeping flute is added to each leaflet (Fig 6.51).

Fig 6.49 Forming the leaflets: those on the left have been stabbed in, those on the right relieved

Fig 6.50 The sharp arris of the corner leaf must appear straight when viewed at 45°

Fig 6.51 The completed capital, showing the leaflets enlivened by simple fluting

Fig 6.52 Pilaster capital modeled on those from the Tower of the Winds in Athens

# PILASTER CAPITAL FROM THE TOWER OF THE WINDS

The Tower of the Winds in Athens (48 BCE) is a wonderful octagonal building, more properly called the Horologium of Andronikos Cyrrhestes after its maker and its original use: it was a weather station having a sundial, weather vane, and water-clock. On the sides are relief carvings depicting the eight winds. Two sides formerly had porticos, the columns of which had capitals combining the palm or stiff leaf with a row of acanthus leaves. This arrangement is not completely unique, but has come down through the ages via the Tower of the Winds capital. Though the originals are in the round, the type is readily adapted to pilasters (Fig 6.52). A simple block can be fabricated and the more detailed leaves can be added to it, as will be explained below. This technique can also be adapted to the more complex Corinthian capitals, described later in this chapter.

## FORMING THE BLANK

First, the width of the base of the blank is determined from the width of the pilaster shaft. The astragal at the base of the capital is used to separate it visually from the column, as well as to cover the joint between the two. The lower part of the capital is flat to accommodate the acanthus leaves, while the flare at the top is somewhat elliptical, making a congé configuration.

Leave enough material in the fillet at the top to allow for the grounding of the stiff leaves. Above the congé there is a molding comprising an undecorated cavetto and ovolo, which serves as the abacus; in our example this is made separately.

Three acanthus leaves, plus the two half-leaves at the corners, will have to fit into the width required (Figs 6.53 and 6.54). The stiff leaves when viewed in elevation seem a little long, but when viewed from below they are partially obscured by the curl of the acanthus leaves, and this puts them back into proportion. There should be a stiff leaf over each acanthus and between each pair of acanthus leaves, making a total of seven whole leaves and two half-leaves at the corners. Depending upon the width of material available, side blocks may have to be added in order to accommodate the corner half-leaves or one full acanthus-leaf width. It does not matter whether the stiff leaves or the acanthus are carved first, but the blanks for the latter must be made to fit the width of the larger blank. These acanthus-leaf blanks can be fabricated from a wide board using a table saw and bandsaw, then cut apart to make the individual leaves (Fig 6.55).

The corner leaves are made in two pieces joined at a 45° miter, and curl outward more than the other leaves (Fig 6.56). Gluing the two halves together prior to carving makes it easier to achieve symmetry, but also makes them more difficult to hold. To surmount

Fig 6.53 Carving sequence: partially finished leaves laid on the shaped blank

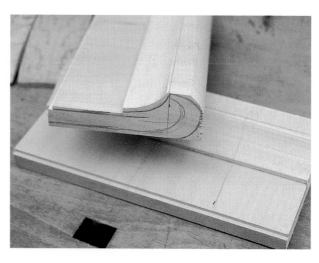

Fig 6.55 Leaf blanks fabricated from wide boards, ready to be cut up into separate leaves

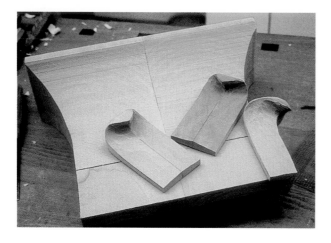

Fig 6.54 The half-leaf at the corner requires a differently shaped blank

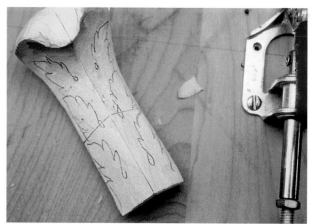

Fig 6.56 The mitered blank for the corner leaf

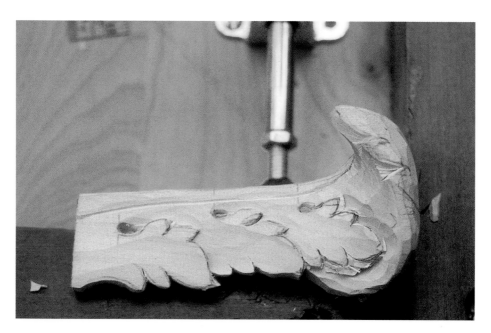

Fig 6.57 A jig consisting of a wooden block and a toggle clamp holds the L-shaped corner leaf during carving

this difficulty, a jig can be made quickly with a supporting block and a toggle clamp, as shown in Fig 6.57; alternatively, the leaves can be temporarily tacked to a larger block.

## CARVING THE LEAVES

The curl of the leaf is defined first, and the broad part of the blank thinned toward the bottom so that there is a gentle sweep from the tip around the curl to the base (Figs 6.58–6.60). Then the leaflets are shaped, set in, and modeled; Fig 6.61 shows the different stages, and 6.62 shows how the back edges are undercut.

*Fig 6.59  Beginning to carve the curl; the sides of the leaf have already been sloped back from the central vein*

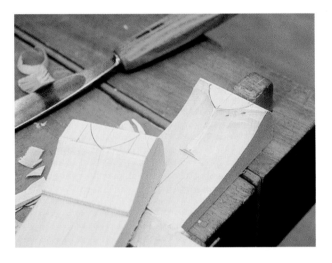

*Fig 6.58  Beginning to carve the leaves: at front, the sawn blank; behind, preliminary shaping with the gouge*

*Fig 6.60  The curl defined and ready for undercutting*

*Fig 6.61  Stages in marking and carving the leaflets; the curl at the top has already been undercut*

Fig 6.62  *The back edges are slightly undercut to give a sense of relief*

*Fig 6.63 Side elevation of the stiff leaf, showing the strengthening rib left underneath when the curl is undercut*

Where the top of the leaf curls forward, a rib-like piece of material is left underneath for strength (Fig 6.63). The curl of the corner leaves will have to be adjusted so that the leaflets lie in the same plane as the front leaves.

The stiff leaves carved on the capital itself consist of a central stem with flutes on either side, similar to those already seen in Fig 6.4 (and, incidentally, very much like the face of the voluted bracket described in Chapter 4). Fig 6.64 shows the layout, and 6.65 the partially carved leaves. The acanthus leaves are glued and nailed (through the eyes) to the blank. The abacus and astragal are added on installation.

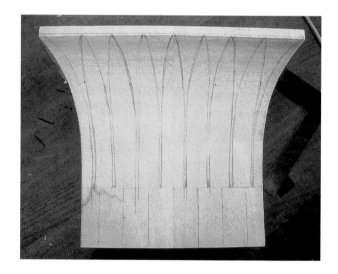

*Fig 6.64  The stiff leaves laid out on the capital blank*

*Fig 6.65  The stiff leaves partially carved; the pencil marking on the uncarved one shows an alternative cross-sectional treatment*

# THE CORINTHIAN CAPITAL

The Corinthian capital is said to have been "invented" by Callimachus when he noticed an acanthus plant sprouting up around a basket. Though no doubt apocryphal, the story illustrates the usual bell-shaped barrel of the capital and the way in which the acanthus leaves seem to grow from the bottom of it. From the double tier of acanthus leaves spring stalks, called *caulicoli*, which end in tight spirals. The corner volutes support the projecting corner of the abacus, while the smaller inner ones meet in the middle, or even interlock arm-in-arm in some examples. Fig 6.66 shows a typical rendition, and 6.67 shows the same design adapted to a square pillar. The caulicoli are often accompanied by sheathlike leaves (see Figs 6.70 and 6.71). In the middle of the abacus there is usually a flower blossom, or **fleuron** (Fig 6.68). Besides their usual association with supporting building superstructures, Corinthian pilasters or half-columns are used to support entablatures over doors and windows, as well as interior cornices; Fig 6.69 shows a wonderful example.

*Fig 6.67 A square version of the same design*

*Fig 6.66 A typical Corinthian capital, at Jefferson's University of Virginia (one corner of the abacus is broken)*

*Fig 6.68 In this example the fleuron in the center of the abacus is made of metal*

123

Fig 6.69  Corinthian half-columns supporting a pediment above a window, Col. John Brice House, Annapolis, MD, 1772

Fig 6.71  A variation on the Corinthian capital, with distinctive configuration of acanthus leaves and applied rosettes; note how the flutes of the columns themselves turn into foliage. St Paul's Episcopal Church, Richmond, VA, 1843–5

Fig 6.70  Corinthian capital built up by applying carvings to a central block, Lenygon Collection (Colonial Williamsburg Foundation/ Frederick Wilbur)

The pilaster capital in Fig 6.70 was made by applying carved pieces to a center block in the same fashion as the Tower of the Winds pilaster just described. The capitals shown in Figs 6.71 and 6.72 are interesting variations, as are the copies of Roman designs in Figs 6.73 and 6.74, incorporating Pegasus and the Imperial eagle. Let's not leave out the Art Deco version in Fig 6.75! The drawing of Renaissance capitals in Fig 6.76 further emphasizes the wide variation to be found within the classical idiom.

*Fig 6.73  Winged horses replace the volutes on this capital of the General Assembly Building, Richmond, VA, modeled on those of the Roman temple of Mars Ultor*

*Fig 6.72  In this variation from Charleston, SC, serried ranks of acanthus leaves almost crowd out the volutes above*

*Fig 6.74  The Roman Imperial eagle adorns an otherwise conventional Corinthian capital on the same building*

*Fig 6.75  Even in this uncompromising Art Deco treatment (in Great Marlborough Street, London), the essential elements of the Corinthian capital are easily recognized*

*Fig 6.76 Fifteenth-century marble capitals, from C. B. Griesbach,* Historic Ornament: A Pictorial Archive *(by courtesy of Dover Publications, Inc.):
(a, b, c) vault consoles from the Ducal Palace, Urbino;
(d, e) capitals from the charterhouse near Florence*

## CARVING A SMALL CORINTHIAN CAPITAL

Fig 6.77 shows a pair of Corinthian half-capitals only 5in (127mm) tall. The carving process is not described in detail here because the approach is similar to those described previously, in that the larger forms are determined and isolated first, followed by the details. Fig 6.78 shows the abacus laid out, 6.79 the underside. Fig 6.80 shows the blocking out of the corner

volutes, the central volutes, and the middle leaf. Figs 6.81 and 6.82 show the corner volutes drawn in and further defined. The acanthus leaves have been sketched on the "bell" of the capital in Fig 6.83. The smaller middle volutes are finished next, and then the caulicoli and acanthus leaves (Fig 6.84). In Fig 6.85 the two finished half-capitals are placed back to back to show what a full column capital in this style would look like.

Fig 6.77  A small pair of Corinthian half-capitals

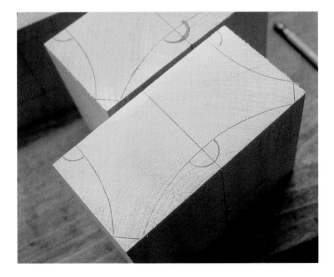

Fig 6.78  The blanks seen from above, with the shape of the abacus marked out

Fig 6.79  The underside of the capital marked out on the blank

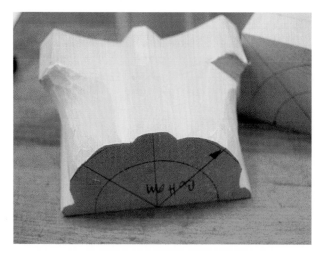

Fig 6.80  The main forms of the capital blocked out

Fig 6.82  Detail of the corner at the same stage

Fig 6.81  The corner volutes marked and further blocked out

Fig 6.83  The corner volutes carved and the principal leaves drawn in

Fig 6.84  The central volutes and caulicoli in place, and the leaves further defined; final detailing of the leaves and rosette is still to be done

*Fig 6.85 The two completed half-capitals*

# THE COMPOSITE CAPITAL

The Composite capital, of which one form is shown in Fig 6.86, combines the Ionic volutes and echinus with the bell shape and double row of acanthus leaves of the Corinthian order.

*Fig 6.86 Composite capital by the author: just one example from the many possible variations*

CHAPTER

# APPLICATIONS

Picture frames • Mantels • Gateposts

I n this concluding chapter, several projects are illustrated which integrate some of the decorative elements discussed in previous chapters. They are relatively easy to make in the modestly equipped shop and with a modicum of carving tools. Moldings can be run with a router and bits or shaped by hand planes, since many moldings can be built up using a combination of smaller profiles. A local cabinet shop may be willing to set up for a short run of moldings, especially if they have the shaper knives you need already ground, or if you are willing to use standard profiles. In my Notes to the Reader it was suggested that the carver design around his or her tools and equipment, so the following projects are not intended to encourage step-by-step copying of a particular piece. Part of the purpose here is to show the construction of the pieces, as well as the options for decoration.

As we have seen, the many ancillary aspects of a classical building are derived from the design of the building itself. Doors and windows often have full entablatures with pediments above. To make a door surround, the architrave of the entablature is turned through 90° and dropped down the sides of the opening, butting onto a plinth at the baseboard (skirting board). A typical door architrave is illustrated in Fig 7.1, consisting of an astragal, a simple cyma, and a backband of small cavetto and ovolo. The decoration depicted is from a fragment in the Lenygon Collection, Colonial Williamsburg. The molding in Fig 2.31 may also have been a door or window architrave.

A mantelpiece can be nearly an exact copy of a door entablature without pediment, creating a mantel which echoes the proportions, or at least the elements,

> *Artists, carvers in particular, are the true scribes and historians of their times.*
>
> GEORGE JACK

of the orders. An Ionic mantel would have a pulvinated frieze, dentils, and even pilaster capitals (see Fig 7.24), while a Doric mantel would have simpler lines, with triglyphs and rosettes in the metopes. The Corinthian capital might be a little too delicate for this use, as the leaf curls could easily be knocked off, and the modillions typical of the order are quite overstated for a mantel shelf, but this is not to say that these elements are not to be found. By extension, picture frames can look strikingly similar to the east elevation of the Erechtheion. Furniture can take on the same aspect by using pilasters with capitals, moldings, pediments with acroteria, and other aspects of the classical Greek or Roman building. The Philadelphia desk and bookcase seen in Fig 1.11 shows a conglomeration of various elements from several orders, including Ionic pilasters and a Doric frieze with rosettes and triglyphs.

## PICTURE FRAMES

The picture frame is a good place for aspiring carvers to start practicing the carving techniques described in this book. The construction of most frames is fairly straightforward, with few complicated joints, but the simple frame can be embellished with some impressive elements. The modern picture frame did not develop until the late medieval period, when altarpieces were painted on wood panels and framed with moldings. Originally, the moldings were either worked into the panel itself before painting, or attached to the panel afterward; the idea of a removable frame came somewhat later. By the sixteenth century the custom of hanging pictures together in a gallery was common in

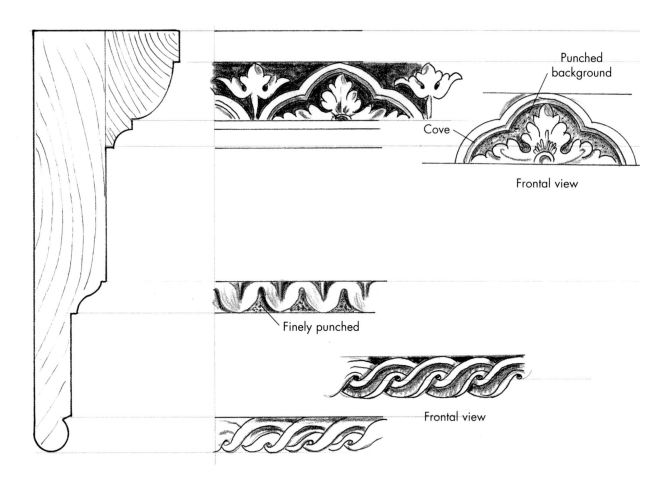

Punched
background

Cove

Frontal view

Finely punched

Frontal view

*Fig 7.1 Sectional drawing of a typical eighteenth-century door architrave, with examples of how the moldings might be decorated. "Frontal" views show how the decoration would look if spread out flat*

the great houses of Europe. The history of picture and mirror frames is an interesting one, involving many artistic subtleties and some controversy: at what point does the frame take on such artistic presence as to shut out the object for which it was created?

Many frames are made up almost entirely from architectural elements. In the case of **tabernacle frames** the temple façade is echoed—and many literally consist of all the elements found in the orders. This style derives from the medieval altarpiece, which was protected from the dust by a tracery canopy (derived, of course, from the elements of the overall structure of the church). The **box frame** or **cassetta** is the familiar rectangular frame consisting of combined moldings. In many instances these moldings remind one of a door or

*Fig 7.2 Italian mirror frame, late seventeenth century, Victoria and Albert Museum (V&A Museum/Frederick Wilbur)*

window architrave with a projecting outer **backband**, a flat frieze, and an inner bead, as in the example about to be described. Sometimes from the outside molding a cavetto descends toward the painting in order to draw in the viewer or prevent the eyes wandering from the picture. The **reverse frame** is more or less opposite to this notion: here the frame takes on the idea of furniture, blending the picture with the wall. In this type of frame the greatest projection is near to the painting, and outer moldings recede backward toward the wall upon which the painting is mounted.

Eighteenth-century frames are often overrun with acanthus fronds, cavorting ho-ho birds, and smiling C-scrolls. Seemingly to accentuate their laciness, they are often pierced to the point of fragility, as can be seen by a quick glance at Thomas Chippendale's mirror

frame designs, or the late seventeenth-century Italian frame in Fig 7.2.

## MAKING AND CARVING A CLASSICAL FRAME

The frame illustrated in Figs 7.3–7.6 begins with a baseboard or field upon which the astragal and ovolo moldings are applied. This is a common arrangement, and the two moldings are often decorated with beads and egg and dart, respectively. Alternative possibilities would be bead and billet with a cyma waterleaf, or small waterleaf with an acanthus cyma. In the crossettes at the bottom are rosettes. This configuration can also be used for overmantel paneling and other situations requiring a frame, including door architraves and fire surrounds. The top of the frame can be left

*Fig 7.3 A crossetted mirror or picture frame, with a pulvinated frieze in the entablature, designed and made by the author after examples of the Empire (Regency) period*

Fig 7.4  A detail of the entablature and crossetted corner

Fig 7.6  Detail of rosette

Fig 7.7  Fitting the astragals to the field, using clothes pins as clamps and a rabetted block to gauge the distance from the edge of the frame

without crossettes, but in this case small console blocks hold up the "ears" (Fig 7.5). The entablature consists of an architrave (which is, of course, the frame itself), a pulvinated frieze decorated with leaves, and a cornice composed of corona and cymatium. A pediment with a cartouche in the tympanum could have been added as well.

To construct a similar frame, first establish the size of the painting or mirror to be framed. (Ready-made frames are of standard sizes.) Subtract from the inside of this rectangle enough to allow for the rabbet which holds the glass or painting. The depth of the rabbet should be determined by the thickness of the object to be held, including any backing material. The field must be thick enough to accommodate this rabbet whilst leaving enough strength to secure the picture or mirror.

Fig 7.5  Detail of console bracket

*Fig 7.8  Carving the astragal beads*

*Fig 7.9  Carving the egg and dart for the backband*

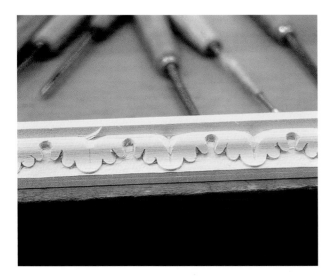

*Fig 7.10  Carving the leaf ornament for the bed molding*

The rectangular shape is best mitered, with the dog-ears and entablature added separately. For large frames, woods such as basswood (lime) or pine reduce the weight and the consequent strain on the hanging hardware. The four mitered pieces can be biscuit-jointed for strength. The moldings to be carved should be run and mitered to fit the frame before carving; they will later be applied directly to the field. The astragal is set in slightly from the inner edge of the frame; it can be spaced from the edge by the simple gauge block shown in Fig 7.7, and held with spring-type clothes pins during fitting and gluing. The backband creating the crossetted frame has 12 inside and 8 outside miters, which require leaves. All the necessary techniques for carving the moldings were covered in Chapters 2 and 3. Figs 7.8–7.10 show the carving in progress.

The rosettes should be sized so that they have plenty of margin—not so large as to fill the space—though there is no rule of thumb. Those shown here can be turned on the lathe and then carved, as Figs 7.11–7.14 illustrate. Note how the petals curl back toward the center disk.

The pulvinated frieze can be thought of as a molding; the surface is carved by the same stab-and-relieve technique, leaving no ground and therefore relatively little depth. After dimensioning the blank in width and thickness, draw the arc on the ends. A hand plane can then be used to round the profile (Fig 7.15). The small facets left by the plane will be carved away in due course. From the centerline, where the ribbons cross, calculate the number of rows of leaves required; Fig 7.16 shows several exploratory drawings, with the chosen version shaded in. Set in the outlines of the

*Fig 7.11  Turning the blank for the rosette; it is held on a woodscrew chuck, using 100-grit sandpaper to prevent it from slipping*

*Fig 7.12  The rosette marked out and the lower petals defined*

*Fig 7.15  Shaping the blank for the frieze by planing down to the curved line marked on the ends*

*Fig 7.13  Setting in the curls of the upper leaves*

leaves, allowing for the berry at the tip of each leaf. Relieve the material at the base of the leaves and carve the berry in the same way as for an astragal bead, that is, with the gouge turned over. Fig 7.17 shows the different stages of this process from left to right; a detail of the completed design is given in Fig 7.18, and the whole frieze is shown in Fig 7.19. The short returns at the ends are left blank, except for a groove parallel to the front surface and ½in (13mm) back from it.

The moldings of the entablature wrap around the sides of the field, and are cut and mitered before carving. As with any built-up entablature, some blocking is needed at the back to support the mitered pieces of molding. Above the cymatium a flat "roof" spans the entire depth of the frame.

*Fig 7.14  The completed rosette*

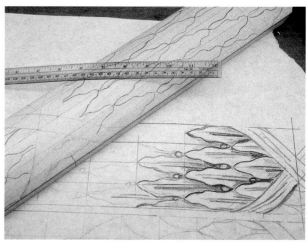

*Fig 7.16  Designing the leaf treatment to be used on the pulvinated frieze*

Fig 7.17  Stages in carving
the frieze

Fig 7.18  A detail of the
completed leaves

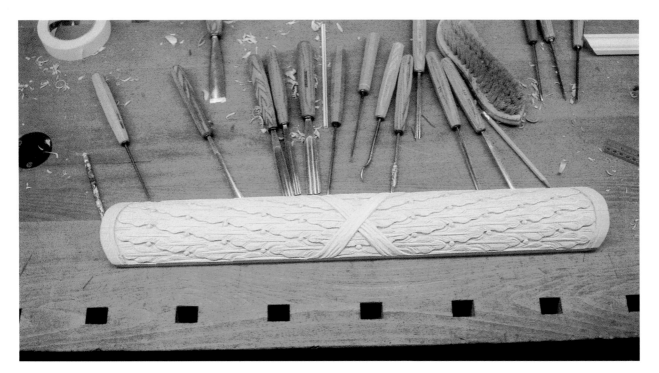

Fig 7.19  The completed frieze, with the tools used to carve it

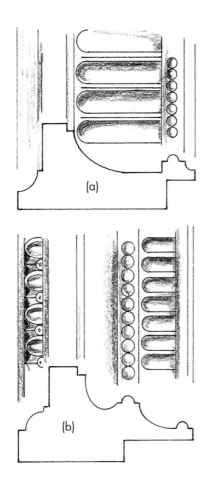

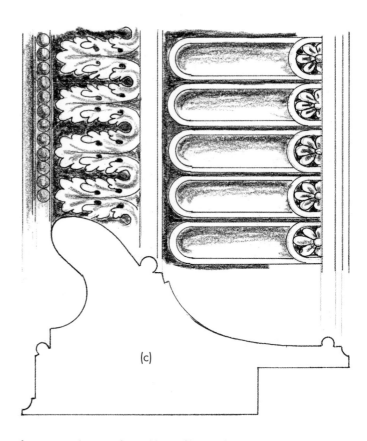

Fig 7.20 (above and opposite) Moldings for box picture frames: a selection of suitable profiles, with suggested decoration

## MAKING A BOX FRAME

The box frame (including the reverse frame) is simply a series of moldings mitered at the corners (Fig 7.20). Many complex profiles can be created from smaller ones. By way of illustration, Fig 7.21 shows a method of constructing the molding shown in Fig 7.20g.

The stock labeled #1 serves as the base to which the smaller pieces are applied. The large cavetto can be made on the table saw by feeding the stock diagonally through the blade. Experimentation with scrap stock is imperative. The intended profile needs to be drawn on the end of the stock; the stock is then set on the saw

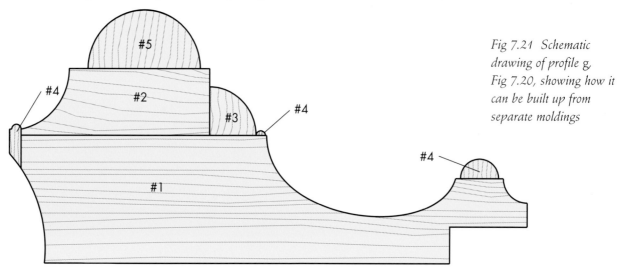

Fig 7.21 Schematic drawing of profile g, Fig 7.20, showing how it can be built up from separate moldings

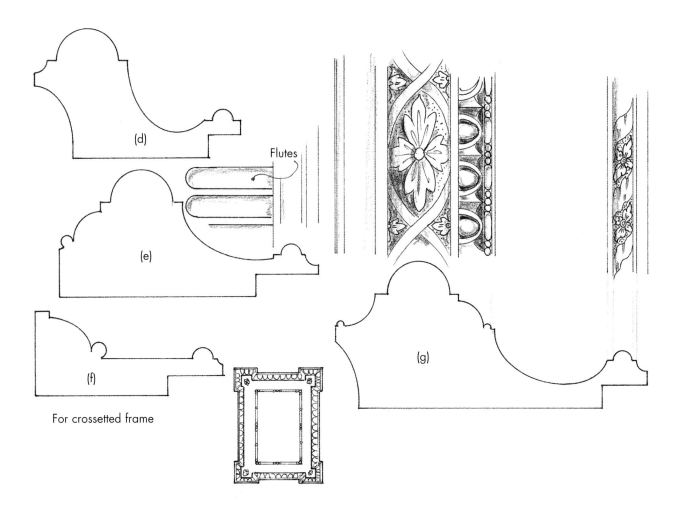

(d)

Flutes

(e)

(f)

For crossetted frame

(g)

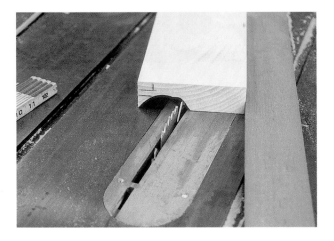

*Fig 7.22 Cutting a cove on the table saw*

table behind the blade, which has been raised to the approximate height (or depth) desired. From the outfeed side of the saw, sight toward the end of the stock. Note how the path of the blade will cut an elliptical groove down the stock, and that adjusting the stock this way and that will alter the shape of the resulting cavetto. Adjust the stock more or less diagonally to the blade to achieve the desired cut. It is better to start with stock wider than the finished size, to ensure sufficient bearing surface during these operations. When a satisfactory ellipse has been found, a fence is clamped to the table top along the edge of the stock (Fig 7.22). To obtain the desired profile it may be necessary to pass the stock through the blade several times with different fence adjustments. In the example shown, two arcs may be used to create the desired ellipse. These two arcs may not neatly merge, and the small peak left between them will need some cleaning up with gouge or scraper; the surface left by the saw blade will have to be smoothed to some degree anyway.

Before cutting begins, the blade is lowered so that only a small fraction of an inch is exposed. Pass all the pieces through the blade before raising it for the next pass. Raise the blade slightly on successive passes until the desired result is obtained. **Be aware that this is a procedure requiring patience and mindfulness—it is potentially very dangerous.** Use featherboards or other hold-downs, and use a push stick rather than feeding the wood by hand. Make sure there will be no distractions during the operation. The base piece is coved in the same way at the outside edge. On the inside edge, rout a small cove and the rabbet for holding the mirror or picture.

The piece labeled #2 is milled next, and the cavetto routed on the outside edge. The ovolo (#3) is made and applied. The small astragals (#4) are then made with the router or beading plane; it is much easier to machine or plane a larger piece and then cut the astragal from it. The bead which is glued to the outside of the frame will have to be "faired in" to the cavetto already cut on the base piece. Alternatively, the second piece and the outside bead could be glued to the base before the outside cove is sawn. The larger astragal (#5) can be made with a quarter-round router bit, if you have one of the correct size, or by hand-planing it round as described above for the pulvinated frieze.

The various moldings can be glued together before mitering or left to be individually mitered after the base piece is assembled, as with the previously described mirror frame. The method chosen may depend upon the capacity of the available equipment. In either case, gauge blocks can be used to position the moldings during glue-up, as with the astragals on the frame described above.

## GILDING

Rarely are picture frames left without a painted or gilded finish. Gilding is an ancient art, beginning at least as early as 2600 BCE in (where else?) Egypt. It has been used for statuary and architectural embellishment throughout the ages.

Early frames were usually without gilding, but as the demand for the finish grew in the eighteenth and nineteenth centuries various economical ways were found to create ornament from other materials than wood, namely composition, plaster, or even embossed paper designs, with sheet lead for leaves, wire for stems, and glass beads for berries. Composition, or "compo", is made of gilder's whiting (powdered chalk), animal-skin glue, linseed oil, and rosin (a resin refined from pine sap); these are mixed to form a putty-like substance which is then pressed into molds for the various ornaments. Gold, of course, can be mixed with other metals, and as it becomes less pure, it becomes paler and less yellow in appearance. Other metals, such as silver, aluminum, and copper, are also rolled or pounded into thin sheets or "leaf".

There are two methods of applying gold leaf to wood surfaces: by using oil-based or water-based adhesive. In oil gilding, a prepared surface is coated with an oil "size" or varnish which, after drying to a slightly tacky surface, acts as the adhesive to hold the thin sheet of gold. In water gilding, the surface is prepared with gesso and followed by bole, which is a fine clay mixed with animal-skin glue. This water-soluble coating, when again moistened, allows for the application of the gold leaf. Because the gesso and bole dry to a fairly hard, smooth surface, the gold coating then can be burnished by rubbing with a hard agate tool, which enhances its reflective properties. The burnished areas contrast with those surfaces which are not

*Fig 7.23 Carved decoration on a flat mantel frieze, Hammond–Harwood House, Annapolis, MD ( Hammond–Harwood House Association/ Frederick Wilbur)*

burnished and remain matt. The gold is protected by a clear top coat, and is often toned with pigments to emphasize the depth of carving. There are a number of handbooks available for those who require more detailed information.

## MANTELS

The purpose of the backband of a mantel is to cover the joint between the masonry of the fireplace and the wall fabric, or between field and wall. Quite often this is the only embellishment to the fireplace but, because the hearth is traditionally the focus of a room (in fact, *focus* is Latin for "hearth"), it is commonly framed and surmounted by a wide array of elements. Naturally the elements which make up the orders, and which were adapted to doors and windows, were just as easily

transformed into the mantelpiece. Above the backband, an entablature holds up the shelf which, after all, is only a flat roof. As with the mirror frame, the field surrounding the opening serves as the architrave, with an inner molding which covers the juncture between the wall and the marble or brick fire surround. The frieze sits on top of this frame, with tiers of moldings projecting outward to make up the cornice which supports the shelf.

The frieze probably displays the most variety, as many decorations can be carved into or applied to it. It can be a flat surface with or without interruptions and decorations (Fig 7.23), or it can be a plain or carved pulvinated frieze. The former usually has some sort of molded border to contain the expanse, or contrasting blocks near the ends (Figs 7.24 and 7.25). These blocks can be either the extension of the pilaster "legs", or

*Fig 7.24 Mantel by the author, with Ionic pilasters, pilaster blocks on frieze, and cartouche with foliage (photograph by Phillip Beaurline)*

Fig 7.25 *Frieze end block with applied rosette, Hammond–Harwood House (Hammond–Harwood House Association/Frederick Wilbur)*

Fig 7.27 *An example with block decoration in the center of the frieze*

Fig 7.26 *Acanthus-leaf console block on the mantel shown in Fig 7.23, Hammond–Harwood House (Hammond–Harwood House Association/Frederick Wilbur)*

Fig 7.28 *Mantelpiece with applied frieze of circular fretwork with rosettes (by courtesy of Mrs James C. Wheat/ Frederick Wilbur)*

Fig 7.29 *Detail of the frieze shown in the previous figure (by courtesy of Mrs James C. Wheat/ Frederick Wilbur)*

*Fig 7.30 Mantel with pulvinated frieze, Hammond–Harwood House (Hammond–Harwood House Association/ Frederick Wilbur)*

console blocks (Fig 7.26). The moldings immediately above the frieze invariably wrap around these interruptions; the corona (that is, the shelf) usually runs straight across the width, though sometimes it also echoes the interruptions, as in several of the examples shown here. Often a rectangular space is set aside in the middle of the frieze to contain a sculptural relief, as in Fig 7.27, or applied ornamentation in the form of fretwork and rosettes, as in Figs 7.28 and 7.29. The pulvinated frieze can be carved with oak or laurel leaves (Figs 7.30 and 7.31). In many instances the console blocks are placed in line with the ends of the entablature (Fig 7.32).

*Fig 7.31 Detail of the frieze shown in the previous figure (Hammond–Harwood House Association/Frederick Wilbur)*

*Fig 7.32 Detail of the mantelpiece illustrated in Fig 7.27, showing a console block or voluted bracket mounted on the side of the backband*

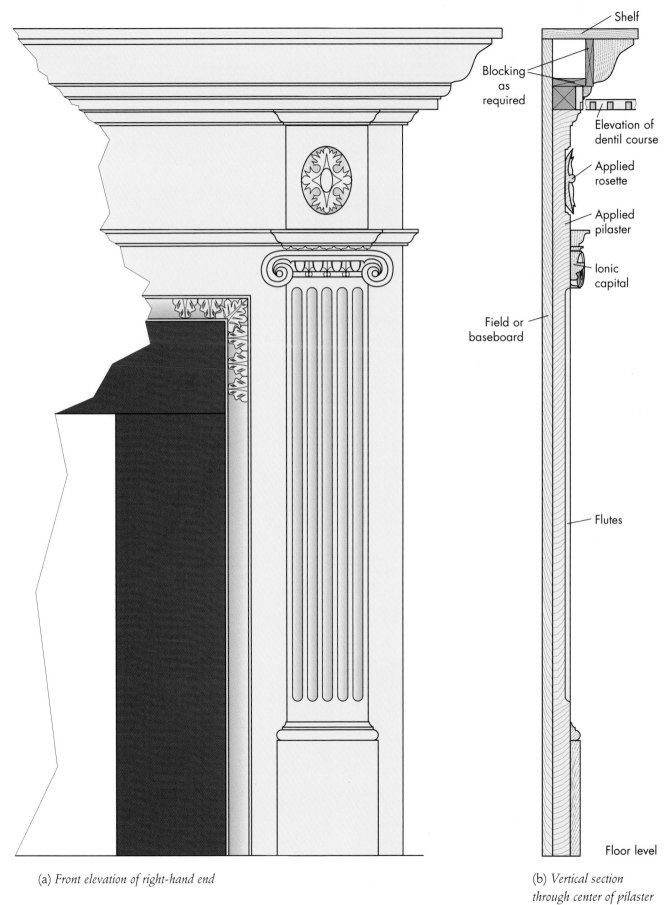

(a) *Front elevation of right-hand end*

(b) *Vertical section through center of pilaster*

*Fig 7.33  Sections and elevations (not to same scale) of the mantel shown in Fig 7.24*

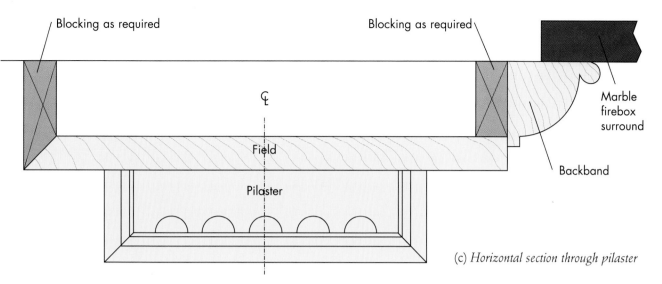

Blocking as required

Blocking as required

Marble
firebox
surround

Backband

Field

Pilaster

(c) *Horizontal section through pilaster*

The series of drawings in Fig 7.33 shows how the mantel in Fig 7.24 (and Fig 2.3) is constructed. The elevation of the right side of the mantel (Fig 7.33*a*) shows the placement of the pilaster in relation to the firebox, as well as the overall appearance of the piece. The vertical section through the pilaster and entablature (Fig 7.33*b*) shows the application of the moldings and the additional blocks necessary to apply them.

The horizontal section through the pilaster (Fig 7.33*c*) shows the spacing and depth of the flutes in the face of the pilaster. Fig 7.33*d* is a detail of the rosettes which are recessed into the frieze blocks (see also Fig 5.28). The rosettes, the pilaster capitals, and all the carved moldings use the techniques described in earlier chapters. Dentils can be cut on the table saw using a finger-joint jig, a technique described by Tage Frid in *Tage Frid Teaches Woodworking*, Book I (Taunton Press, 1979), page 90. Flutes can be run with a core-box bit in the router.

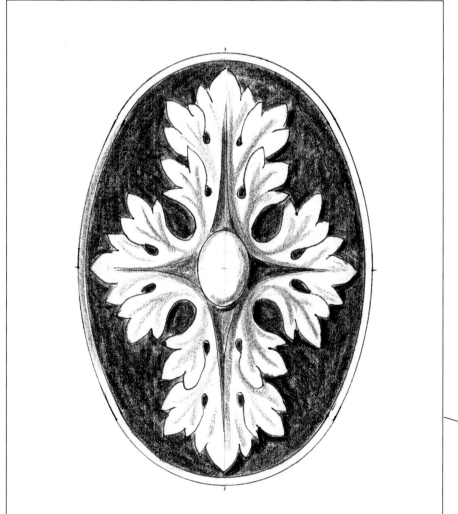

Edge of block

(d) *Applied rosette (see Fig 5.28 for photograph)*

# GATEPOSTS

For all the attention architects have given to columns and their characteristics, there are few uses for free-standing, non-architectural ones. Trajan's Column in Rome may be said to be architectural, but gate and fence posts are more functional! Columnar forms have been adapted to smaller objects such as candlesticks, lampposts, parking stanchions (bollards), table pedestals, and the like (Figs 7.34 and 7.35).

The post illustrated in Fig 7.36 makes use of Doric metopes and triglyphs as well as acanthus-leaved console brackets on two sides (Fig 7.37). It is finished off with a pineapple finial. The making of a similar finial (though without the metal leaves) is described in my article in *Woodcarving* magazine #41 (May/June 1998), pages 53–7. Many posts terminate in finials, the varieties of which are numerous, from pinecones and flames to baskets of fruit and draped urns.

*Fig 7.34 Lamppost outside Jefferson's Virginia State Capitol building, using (from top to bottom) acanthus leaves, stiff leaf, guilloche astragal, stiff leaf, and egg and dart*

The gatepost of Figs 7.38 and 7.39 has a generally classical feel, but is not a strict interpretation of any order. There are suggestions of an entablature, but it is abbreviated. The pillar sits on a square plinth and has a base consisting of a reed and ribbon torus and a simple waterleaf cyma reversa. It is interrupted near the top by a cavettto and gadrooned necking. Above a square architrave is another cavetto and a band carved with rosettes and flutes mimicking the Doric frieze. This band also looks suspiciously like a corona which supports the enlarged cymatium.

The post is essentially a square tube, mitered and splined at the corners. This type of construction has several advantages over a solid post: it is dimensionally more stable, and the interior space makes for easier installation and wiring if the post is to incorporate an electric lamp. In designing the post, attention should be given to the quiet ravaging which the weather will unleash upon it. Any exterior construction experiences a difference in exposure from one side to the other, so it is best to plan for expansion and contraction, proper drainage, and protective finish. It will be necessary to use chemically treated wood, or a particularly durable timber such as redwood, cedar, or cypress, for the basic structure. Waterproof or epoxy glue should be used, as well as galvinized

*Fig 7.35 Post using various leaves, flutes, egg and dart, anthemion, beads (V&A Museum/Frederick Wilbur)*

brads or stainless-steel screws. The carvings should be designed as much as possible to shed water: hence the large cymatium and the gadrooned necking whose natural shape aids water run-off (cavettos are appropriate as well). The roof is sloped for the same reason, and should be covered with copper or other sheet metal.

Fig 7.36 Gatepost with pineapple finial and console brackets at the sides (by courtesy of Charles J. Stick)

Fig 7.37 Detail of the same gatepost, showing the console bracket (by courtesy of Charles J. Stick) (see also Fig 1.23)

Fig 7.38 Gatepost with classical features, by the author

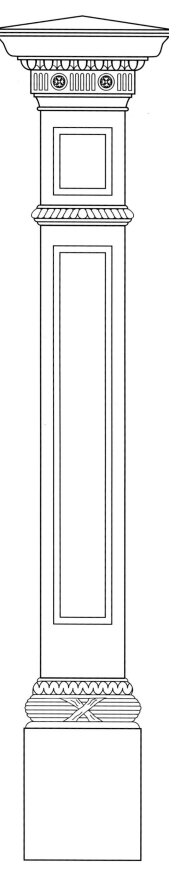

Fig 7.39 Elevation of the gatepost shown in the previous figure

Fig 7.40 *The method of attaching the top to the square tube*

Fig 7.41 *Planing the torus to shape*

The box should be as square as possible, because of the many miters which wrap around it. The roof is fixed with a block which fits snugly inside the tube, as shown in Fig 7.40; screws then pass into the block through the tube. Profile the moldings and fit them temporarily with brads. After labeling, remove and carve them. Figs 7.41–7.44 show the torus molding being carved. Though in real life a ribbon tied around reeds would tend to bend them inward, for decorative purposes this is not desirable. The ribbons should be defined and the area to be reeded taken down to a uniform depth between the ribbons and the miter. Obviously, the reeds should match at the miter; though some reeded friezes have leaves at the miters, it is not advantageous here. The idea is to replicate the torus

Fig 7.42 *Setting in the ribbon on the planed surface*

Fig 7.43 *Marking out the parallel reeds using a plastic grid intended for quilters*

base of a column, so anything which helps to create that illusion is desirable.

Figs 7.45 and 7.46 show the flutes and rosettes on the frieze being carved. When laying out the flutes, the outermost ones should be set well back from the miter, because carving too deeply would break the fragile edge of the material. The rosettes are set in and the background then routed for greater shadow. Remember that the carvings should be simple and deep, so that they have definition even in bright sun or after a few coats of paint.

Laying out the gadroon is easy in that only a constant increment is needed. There are still a couple of refinements to be considered, however. The center lobe needs to be a little wider than the running increment in order to get the diagonal set up correctly. The last half-increment at the miter should be increased somewhat as well, because it appears to project further than the others; when viewed from the corner, the oppositely running curves make a shape like the bottom half of an hourglass. If the increment for the diagonal lobes is ¾in (19mm), the center one should be 1in (25mm) wide; the miter unit should be ½in (13mm) instead of the expected ⅜in (10mm).

To carve the gadroon, the front lobes are defined by stabbing in a stop cut at the increment line and then

*Fig 7.44
Carving of reeds
complete; note
the modest but
effective surface
detailing on the
ribbons*

*Fig 7.45 Layout and carving of the flutes and rosettes;
the left-hand rosette in the foreground has been grounded
out with the router*

*Fig 7.46 The completed frieze*

rounding the "nose" of the molding on what will be the front surface of the finished piece (Fig 7.47). Alternatively, if the gadroons die into a ground (as in Figs 2.70 and 2.71), these lobes can be shaped by an appropriate gouge, stabbed perpendicularly to the ground. Next, using a modestly curved gouge such as a #5, stab the sweeping line denoting the valleys between lobes on the top surface of the molding, placing one wing of the tool at the nosing and the other against the wall of the back fillet (Fig 7.48). Finally, working exclusively with gouges turned bevel-side up, the lobes are rounded. In order to follow the grain, it is necessary to work in both directions: outward from the fillet and inward from the nosing back to the fillet (Figs 7.49–7.51). Mounting the work close to the edge of the bench, as in Fig 7.52, makes approaching the

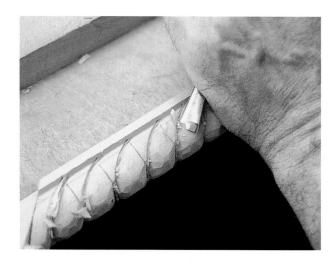

Fig 7.49 Rounding the outer side of each lobe, working away from the fillet

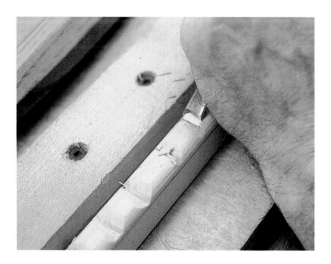

Fig 7.47 Rounding the lobes of the gadroon along the front (upright) edge of the molding

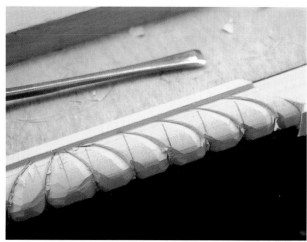

Fig 7.50 Rounding process completed on the outer sides of the lobes

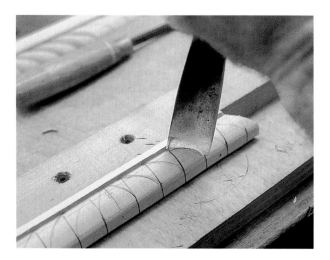

Fig 7.48 Setting in the valleys on the top surface of the gadroon

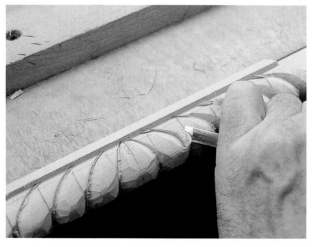

Fig 7.51 Rounding the inner sides of the lobes, working toward the fillet

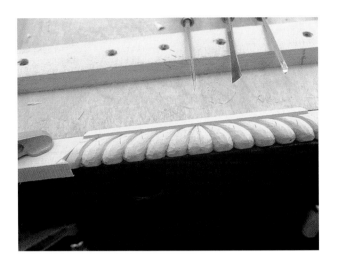

*Fig 7.52 The completed gadroon, showing a convenient method of mounting the work on the edge of the bench*

front of the lobe a little easier; note in this photograph the small blocks holding the workpiece in place. The valleys can be cleaned up with a small parting tool.

The flat surfaces of the post are broken up by the applied astragal molding which suggests frame and panel construction. Sometimes, and erroneously, these are called bolection moldings; they are better described as cock beads with fillets. (A bolection molding is one which acts as a transition from one level to another, as in some panel moldings; hence the confusion. Part of the bolection is proud of the rails and stiles, but on one side it steps down to hold the panel—which means that the back of the molding has a rabbet.)

The easiest way to install the gatepost is to slip it over a second post which has been dimensioned slightly smaller than the interior of the gatepost. Fasten it with screws so that it clears the ground by an inch (25mm) or so. Placing it directly on the ground or on a cement base invites rot. The base can be surrounded by gravel for drainage and ease of maintenance, or mulched and planted with colorful flowers. The gate hinges are then screwed into the inner post through the outer one.

As for finish, there is nothing better than paint. Cracks between moldings, or knots or other flaws, can be filled with auto-body filler, a two-part mix which cures quickly, can be easily sanded when dry, and is paintable. After appropriate sanding of all parts, use a good-quality primer. The two finish coats should be oil-based gloss exterior paint. A brushed finish not only deposits a thicker coating of paint, but also gives the piece a subtle character. Though spraying might seem more efficient, that method does not reach into the

recesses of the carving. Use several different-sized brushes; reaching and cleaning out the crevices of the carving will require a small artist's brush. Use a drinking straw to blow out any paint trapped in small holes.

As with any exterior woodwork, periodic inspection for cracks, dents, and mildew is wise, as catching problems early will save the work. A periodic scrub with mild dish detergent should keep it looking presentable (Fig 7.53).

*Fig 7.53 Regular cleaning and occasional repainting will keep the gatepost in good condition for many years to come*

In any project, whether a fine piece of furniture or an exterior building detail, there is a long tradition of proportion and ornament with which, I hope, the cabinetmaker or architectural carver is now more familiar. Though it has been stressed that the tradition is an enduring one, the variety of examples included here illustates the degree of creativity allowed within it. From understanding comes confidence and experimentation.

# GLOSSARY

This is a listing of words denoted in bold type in the text. The reader is referred to the *Illustrated Dictionary of Historic Architecture* by Cyril M. Harris for a more complete listing.

**abacus** the top member of a capital, which supports the **architrave** or beams of the superstructure of a building.

**acroterion** an ornament placed on a pedestal at the peak or end of a **pediment**.

**ancon** a bracket, usually on a door or window **architrave** (casing), which serves to support the **entablature** or **pediment** above.

**antefix** a **palmette** ornament on the edge of a roof, covering the end of a tile.

**anthemion** the running honeysuckle and palmette design often used on a **frieze** or a **cymatium**.

**applied (appliqué)** (of a molding or other ornament): made separately and subsequently attached to the item to be ornamented, as opposed to being carved **in the solid**.

**architrave** the beams of the superstructure of the roof which rest on the **abacus** of the columns, forming the lowest member of the **entablature**; also a term for door and window casings.

**arcuation** the system of using arches and vaults for support, as opposed to posts and beams (**trabeation**).

**arris** the corner made by planes at 90° to one another, or by a curve meeting a flat plane, e.g. a flute meeting a fillet, or a flute meeting another flute as on a **Doric** column.

**astragal** a small half-round molding, usually embellished with carving.

**Attic base** a column base, usually associated with the Ionic and Corinthian orders, consisting of **tori** with a **scotia** in between.

**backband** a **fillet** (usually found in conjunction with other profiles) at the outer edge of a door, window, or mantel architrave where it returns toward the wall.

**baluster** the roll on either side of an Ionic capital connecting the **volutes**, or the similar feature between volutes on a bracket.

**bead** general term for the **astragal** molding in its many different uses; also, a hemispherical dome carved on an astragal molding.

**bead and billet** a design carved on the **astragal** molding, consisting of groups of hemispherical beads alternating with elongated cylinders.

**bead and reel** a design carved on the **astragal** molding, consisting of hemispherical beads and concave-shaped reels.

**bed molding** the molding between the **frieze** and the **corona** on the **entablature**.

**blank** a piece of wood already shaped and ready for carving.

**bolection** any molding which covers a joint between pieces on different levels and projects from the surface; often used to hold panels into a frame.

**box frame** an ordinary rectangular picture frame composed of molded elements.

**bucranium** a stylized representation of a bull's head or skull

**cable** a molding representing the twists of a rope; also known as **rope** molding.

**cartoon** a drawing, especially a full-sized one, of ornamentation to be carved.

**cartouche** a tablet with scrolled edges.

**cassetta** another term for **box frame**.

**cavetto** a concave quarter-round or quarter-ellipse molding, also called a **cove**.

**chip-carving** the technique of incising pyramidal and similar shapes into the surface to form decorative designs.

**cock bead** a small **bead** which is raised above the surrounding ground.

**congé** a flat vertical surface easing into a concave curve along a length of molding.

**console** general term for a bracket which acts as a support.

**corbel** a support projecting from a wall to carry a beam, arch, or vault.

**cornice** the uppermost member of the **entablature**, consisting of **corona** and **cymatium**.

**corona** part of the **cornice**: the projecting **soffit** above the **frieze**, supporting the **cymatium**.

**cove** a concave molding; a **cavetto**.

**crepidoma** the stepped platform that supports a Greek temple.

**crossette** a projection of the lintel beam past the door posts; any **architrave** which has such a projection. Some picture frames and overmantels have double crossettes, with both members overlapping at the corner.

**cyma recta** a convex–concave molding.

**cyma reversa** a concave–convex molding.

**cymatium** the uppermost member of the **cornice**, usually a **cyma recta** or **ovolo** molding.

**dentil** a small square block, a row of which appears between **frieze** and **corona** in the Ionic and Corinthian orders; the name comes from the Latin for "tooth".

**design** a two-dimensional drawing or **cartoon** of the proposed ornamentation.

**echinus** the bulging part of the Doric capital, which supports the **abacus**.

**egg and dart** an ornament consisting of alternating egg-like and dart-like shapes, used chiefly on the **ovolo** molding.

**elevation** a drawing which shows one of the vertical sides of an object or building.

**entablature** the superstructure of a building, which supports the roof, and consists of **architrave**, **frieze**, and **cornice**; also similar decorative structures above doors, windows, mantels, etc.

**entasis** a slight outward bulge or convexity in the profile of a column, to prevent it from appearing concave to the eye.

**fan** a semicircular ornament consisting of radiating **flutes.**

**fascia** each of the three flat divisions of the **architrave** in the Ionic and Corinthian orders.

**fillet** a narrow flat-faced molding, used to set off other profiles or make transitions between them.

**fleuron** the flower in the middle of the **abacus** of the Corinthian, Composite, and some later versions of the Ionic capital.

**flute** a concave groove, usually arranged in groups, as on column or **pilaster** shafts or flat and concave surfaces.

**fret** a flat, geometric design, such as the **Greek key**.

**frieze** the middle member of the **entablature**; by extension, any wide horizontal band set off by moldings.

**gadrooning** an ornament comprising a series of lobe-like shapes; on a convex molding it takes the form of sweeping teardrops.

**Greek key** a fret design composed of **fillets** meeting at right angles.

**grounding** the background of a relief.

**guilloche** a linear design of interwoven rings.

**in the solid** carved from one piece, as opposed to being carved separately and then **applied**.

**keystone** the wedge-shaped stone or brick, often decorated, at the apex of an arch.

**layout** the process of transferring guidelines and design, by means of a **pattern**, to the material to be carved.

**leaf and dart** an ornament resembling the **waterleaf**, carved on the **cyma recta** molding.

**medallion** a plaque depicting a human head or other isolated object.

**metopes** the flat surfaces in a Doric **frieze**, said to represent the spaces between roof beams (**triglyphs**).

**modeling** shaping the surface of the material to create undulations, especially to depict natural forms such as leaves.

**modillions** the **console** blocks which support the **corona** in the Corinthian order.

**module** a standard unit of comparison and measurement; in the classical orders, the diameter (or in some cases half the diameter) of the column at its base, divided when necessary into smaller units called *minutes*.

**naos** the main compartment or room of a Greek temple.

**necking** a narrow molding between the capital and shaft of a column.

**ogee** a reversing curve, whether in plan, elevation, or section; often used generically for the **cyma recta** and **cyma reversa**.

**ovolo** a convex molding, a quarter-circle or quarter-ellipse in section, often decorated with **egg and dart** design.

**palmette** an ornament derived from a stylized palm leaf.

**patera** a simple **rosette**, usually in a spaced series along an **architrave**.

**pattern** the template or stencil used to transfer the **design** to the material.

**pediment** a low-pitched gable supported by columns and an **entablature**, and sometimes surmounted by **acroteria**.

**pilaster** a shallow pier or rectangular column attached to a wall, with the same decoration as a free-standing column.

**plan** a drawing showing the "footprint" of a building or element thereof; a view from above.

**profile** the shape of the prominent side of an object, such as a molding.

**proportion** the equality of two ratios; more generally, "a correspondence among the measures of the members of an entire work, and of the whole to a certain part selected as standard" (Vitruvius).

**pulvinated** literally "pillow-like"; the term is used primarily to describe a convex **frieze**.

**quirked** (of a molding, such as a quirked bead): having a deep valley between the major **profile** and the adjacent **fillet** or surrounding surface.

**reflected plan** a view of an object from below.

**reverse frame** a type of picture frame in which the greatest projection is adjacent to the inner edge, and the molding recedes toward the wall.

**rinceau** a complex design of swirling acanthus or other leaves.

**rope** another name for the **cable** molding.

**rosette** a round or oval depiction of a stylized flower and/or foliage, with elements radiating from the center.

**scotia** a concave molding consisting of two differing radii.

**scroll** the general term for a spiraling plane.

**section** a drawing of an object as though it has been cut through.

**soffit** the underside of any architectural member.

**spiral** the general word for a circular line made of arcs with diminishing radii.

**stylobate** the "floor" of a temple; the upper surface of the **crepidoma**.

**sunburst** a round or oval ornament formed of radiating reeds.

**tabernacle frame** a frame consisting of **pilasters** or columns with an **entablature** and **pediment**, used to surround a mirror or picture or an architectural element such as a door, window, or niche.

**torus** a large half-round molding, associated with the bases of columns.

**trabeation** the post-and-beam system of construction as used in Greek temples.

**triglyphs** the grooved blocks on the Doric **frieze**, said to represent beam ends.

**tympanum** the triangular area or field enclosed by the moldings of a **pediment**.

**vesica piscis** the shape created by two opposing and intersecting arcs, resembling an American football or a rugby ball.

**volute** the spiral form associated with the Ionic capital and also used for various brackets and scrolls.

**waterleaf** a simple leaf design, usually carved on the **cyma recta** profile.

**wave** a semi-spiral ornament used on flat bands.

# SELECT BIBLIOGRAPHY

There has been a proliferation of carving books in recent years and, though some are valuable resources, the subject matter of many is extremely specialized and has little bearing on architectural carving. Of the six books I reviewed for *Fine Woodworking* magazine in 1979, two are still the best general instructional books on the market. The age-old art of woodcarving hasn't changed much! These are: Paul Hasluck's *Manual of Traditional Woodcarving* and William Wheeler and Charles Hayward's *Woodcarving*. The books by Frederick Brunner mentioned in the review are still very useful to the novice carver.

One recent publication which must be considered the definitive book about tools is Chris Pye's *Woodcarving Tools, Materials & Equipment*. Most authors (or their publishers) seem to feel that their books must include discussions of tools, sharpening, and materials. To most sincerely interested readers this redundancy from book to book becomes annoying. Purchase this one and skip the others.

Sir Banister Fletcher's *History of Architecture on the Comparative Method*, now in its 20th edition, is the best overall history and a fine source for architectural details clearly and exhaustively illustrated. One book directed exclusively at classical architecture is Robert Adam's *Classical Architecture*. Though at times somewhat brief in explanation, this book has abundant illustrations, very clearly rendered. It is not primarily a history but an explanation. Robert Chitham's book *The Classical Orders of Architecture* is an exhaustive comparison between the orders as presented by Vitruvius, Serlio, Vignola, Palladio, Scamozzi, Perrault, and Gibbs. *Classical Architecture* by Demetri Porphyrios is a collection of four fascinating essays about the relevance of the classical tradition to contemporary building; but more than this, it captures the spirit of the classical world in a way histories, dictionaries, and pattern books don't.

Dover Publications Inc. of New York has an extensive list of books on architecture and ornament, and a catalogue should be ordered. They have reprinted most of the major publications on architecture and many design collections and glossaries. One very good glossary is Cyril M. Harris's *Illustrated Dictionary of Historic Architecture*. Meyer's *Handbook of Ornament* must be mentioned because it addresses ornament by various categories: geometric elements (bands, enclosed ornament, etc.), natural forms, and artificial objects (vases, furniture, jewelry). The illustrations include layout lines to show how most designs are drawn. Phillipa Lewis and Gillian Darley's *Dictionary of Ornament* should also be consulted as it has entries which the others do not have, as well as much valuable cross-referencing.

The following, with dates of original publication in parentheses, are all published by Dover. Many are classics which need little introduction.

Alberti, Leon Battista. *The Ten Books of Architecture: The 1755 Leoni Edition*. (1485) 1986.

Benjamin, Asher. *The American Builder's Companion*. (1827) 1969.

—— *The Architect, or Practical House Carpenter*. (1830) 1988.

Chippendale, Thomas. *The Gentleman and Cabinet-Maker's Director*. (1762) 1966.

Cole, Rex Vicat. *Perspective for Artists*. (1921) 1976.

Ghyka, Matila. *The Geometry of Art and Life*. 1977.

Gloag, John. *The Victorian Cabinet-Maker's Assistant*. (1853) 1970.

Griesbach, C. B. *Historic Ornament: A Pictorial Archive*. 1975.

Harris, Cyril M. *Illustrated Dictionary of Historic Architecture*. 1977.

Hasluck, Paul N. (ed.). *Manual of Traditional Wood Carving*. (1911) 1971.

Huntley, H. E. *The Divine Proportion*. 1970.

Meyer, Franz Sales. *Handbook of Ornament*, 4th edn. (1892) 1957.

Palladio, Andrea. *The Four Books of Architecture*, ed. Isaac Ware. (1570/1738) 1965.

Reed, Henry Hope. *Palladio's Architecture and its Influence*. 1980.

Ruskin, John. *The Elements of Drawing*. (1857) 1971.

Serlio, Sebastiano. *The Five Books of Architecture*. (Reprint of English edition of 1611) 1982.

Speltz, Alexander. *The Styles of Ornament*. (Reprint of German edition of 1906) 1959.

Stella, Jacques. *Baroque Ornament and Designs*. 1987.

Vitruvius (M. Vitruvius Pollio). *The Ten Books of Architecture*, trans. Morris Hickey Morgan. 1960.

Ware, William. *The American Vignola*. (1903) 1994.

The following are cited in the text or have been consulted:

Adam, Robert. *Classical Architecture*. New York: Harry N. Abrams, 1990.

Amery, Colin (ed.). *Three Centuries of Architectural Craftsmanship*. London: Butterworth–Heinemann, 1988.

—— *Period Houses and their Details*. London: Butterworth–Heinemann, 1992.

Bates, Elizabeth Bidwell, and Fairbanks, Jonathan L. *American Furniture: 1620–Present*. New York: Richard Marek, 1981.

Bigelow, Deborah, et al. *Gilded Wood: Conservation and History*. Madison, CT: Sound View Press, 1991.

Brownwell, Charles E., et al. *The Making of Virginia Architecture*. Richmond, VA: Virginia Museum of Fine Arts Publications, 1992.

Brunner, Frederick. *Manual of Wood Carving and Wood Sculpture,* 2 vols. Westwood, MA: the author, 1972, 1978.

Chitham, Robert. *The Classical Orders of Architecture*. New York: Rizzoli International, 1985.

Edwards, Betty. *Drawing on the Right side of the Brain*. Los Angeles: J. P. Tracher, 1979.

Esterly, David. *Grinling Gibbons and the Art of Carving*. London: V&A Publications, 1998.

Fletcher, Sir Banister. *A History of Architecture on the Comparative Method*, 20th edn., ed. Dan Cruickshank and Andrew Saint. Oxford: Architectural Press, 1996.

Frid, Tage. *Tage Frid Teaches Woodworking*, Book I. Newtown, CT: Taunton Press, 1979.

Hayward, Charles H. *English Period Furniture*. London: Evans Brothers, 1977.

Hendenryk, Henry. *The Art and History of Frames: An Inquiry into the Enchantment of Painting*. New York: Lyons & Burford, 1963.

Jack, George. *Wood Carving: Design and Workmanship*. (1903). London: Pitman, 1978.

Janson, H. W. *History of Art*, 11th edn. Englewood Cliffs, NJ: Prentice–Hall, 1967.

Krenov, James. *The Fine Art of Cabinetmaking*. New York: Van Nostrand Reinhold, 1975.

Lewis, Phillippa, and Darley, Gillian. *Dictionary of Ornament*. London: Cameron, 1986.

L'Orange, H. P. *Art Forms and Civic Life in the Late Roman Empire*. Princeton University Press, 1972.

Murray, Peter. *The Architecture of the Italian Renaissance*. New York: Schocken/London: Thames and Hudson, 1986 (first pub. London: Batsford, 1963).

Onians, Dick. *Essential Woodcarving Techniques*. Lewes, East Sussex: GMC Publications, 1997.

Oughton, Frederick. *Grinling Gibbons and the English Woodcarving Tradition*. Fresno, CA: Linden Publishing, 1999 (first pub. London: Stobart & Son, 1979).

Parissen, Steven. *Adam Style*. London: Phaidon, 1996.

Penny, Nicholas. *Frames*. London: National Gallery Publications, 1997.

Porphyrios, Demetri. *Classical Architecture*. Windsor, Berks.: Andras Papadakis, 1998.

Pye, Chris. *Woodcarving Tools, Materials & Equipment*. Lewes, East Sussex: GMC Publications, 1994.

Summerson, John. *The Architecture of the Eighteenth Century*. London: Thames and Hudson, 1986.

Tadgell, Christopher. *A History of Architecture,* vols. ii and iv. New York: Watson–Guptil, 1998.

Tavernor, Robert. *Palladio and Palladianism*. London: Thames and Hudson, 1991.

Tomlinson, R. A. *Greek and Roman Architecture*. London: British Museum Press, 1995.

Wharton, Edith, and Codman, Ogden, Jr. *The Decoration of Houses*. (1902) New York: W. W. Norton, 1978.

Wheeler, William, and Hayward, Charles. *Woodcarving*. New York: Drake, 1976.

Woodford, Susan. *The Parthenon*. Cambridge University Press, 1981.

# ABOUT THE AUTHOR

Fred Wilbur is a traditional decorative woodcarver, specializing in architectural elements, furniture components, and wood graphics. He has received commissions from architects, designers, millwork companies, churches, and individuals across America. He has contributed to the restoration of many important national landmarks, including the University of Virginia, Foley Square Courthouse in New York, and the Library of Congress. His work is found in many modern structures as well.

His lifelong interest in the visual and literary arts is supported by degrees from the University of Virginia and the University of Vermont. He has written articles for *Fine Woodworking, American Woodworker, Woodwork,* and *Woodcarving,* and continues to write poetry and publish in literary journals.

Participating in the archaeological excavations at Winchester, England in the late sixties influenced Fred's interest in architecture, scientific method, and the decorative arts. His study and practice of Buddhism continues to influence his approach to both craftsmanship and business. A deep appreciation of the natural world stems from many sources, not the least of which is his early-morning walks under the stars.

He lives with Elizabeth, his wife of thirty years, in the Blue Ridge Mountains of Virginia. She is a dedicated schoolteacher and quilt-maker.

They have two daughters who are also practicing artisans: Heather is currently studying interior design, while Jessica is involved with Renaissance and medieval studies.

# METRIC CONVERSION TABLE

INCHES TO MILLIMETERS AND CENTIMETERS

| in | mm | cm | in | cm | in | cm |
|-----|-----|-----|-----|------|-----|-------|
| ⅛ | 3 | 0.3 | 9 | 22.9 | 30 | 76.2 |
| ¼ | 6 | 0.6 | 10 | 25.4 | 31 | 78.7 |
| ⅜ | 10 | 1.0 | 11 | 27.9 | 32 | 81.3 |
| ½ | 13 | 1.3 | 12 | 30.5 | 33 | 83.8 |
| ⅝ | 16 | 1.6 | 13 | 33.0 | 34 | 86.4 |
| ¾ | 19 | 1.9 | 14 | 35.6 | 35 | 88.9 |
| ⅞ | 22 | 2.2 | 15 | 38.1 | 36 | 91.4 |
| 1 | 25 | 2.5 | 16 | 40.6 | 37 | 94.0 |
| 1¼ | 32 | 3.2 | 17 | 43.2 | 38 | 96.5 |
| 1½ | 38 | 3.8 | 18 | 45.7 | 39 | 99.1 |
| 1¾ | 44 | 4.4 | 19 | 48.3 | 40 | 101.6 |
| 2 | 51 | 5.1 | 20 | 50.8 | 41 | 104.1 |
| 2½ | 64 | 6.4 | 21 | 53.3 | 42 | 106.7 |
| 3 | 76 | 7.6 | 22 | 55.9 | 43 | 109.2 |
| 3½ | 89 | 8.9 | 23 | 58.4 | 44 | 111.8 |
| 4 | 102 | 10.2 | 24 | 61.0 | 45 | 114.3 |
| 4½ | 114 | 11.4 | 25 | 63.5 | 46 | 116.8 |
| 5 | 127 | 12.7 | 26 | 66.0 | 47 | 119.4 |
| 6 | 152 | 15.2 | 27 | 68.6 | 48 | 121.9 |
| 7 | 178 | 17.8 | 28 | 71.1 | 49 | 124.5 |
| 8 | 203 | 20.3 | 29 | 73.7 | 50 | 127.0 |

# INDEX

# TITLES AVAILABLE FROM
# GMC PUBLICATIONS

## BOOKS

### WOODCARVING

| | |
|---|---|
| Beginning Woodcarving | *GMC Publications* |
| Carving Architectural Detail in Wood: | |
| The Classical Tradition | *Frederick Wilbur* |
| Carving Birds & Beasts | *GMC Publications* |
| Carving the Human Figure: | |
| Studies in Wood and Stone | *Dick Onians* |
| Carving Nature: Wildlife Studies in Wood | *Frank Fox-Wilson* |
| Carving on Turning | *Chris Pye* |
| Celtic Carved Lovespoons: 30 Patterns | *Sharon Littley & Clive Griffin* |
| Decorative Woodcarving (New Edition) | *Jeremy Williams* |
| Elements of Woodcarving | *Chris Pye* |
| Essential Woodcarving Techniques | *Dick Onians* |
| Figure Carving in Wood: Human and Animal Forms | *Sara Wilkinson* |
| Lettercarving in Wood: A Practical Course | *Chris Pye* |
| Relief Carving in Wood: A Practical Introduction | *Chris Pye* |
| Woodcarving for Beginners | *GMC Publications* |
| Woodcarving Made Easy | *Cynthia Rogers* |
| Woodcarving Tools, Materials & Equipment | |
| (New Edition in 2 vols.) | *Chris Pye* |

### WOODTURNING

| | |
|---|---|
| Bowl Turning Techniques Masterclass | *Tony Boase* |
| Chris Child's Projects for Woodturners | *Chris Child* |
| Contemporary Turned Wood: New Perspectives in | |
| a Rich Tradition | *Ray Leier, Jan Peters & Kevin Wallace* |
| Decorating Turned Wood: | |
| The Maker's Eye | *Liz & Michael O'Donnell* |
| Green Woodwork | *Mike Abbott* |
| Intermediate Woodturning Projects | *GMC Publications* |
| Keith Rowley's Woodturning Projects | *Keith Rowley* |
| Making Screw Threads in Wood | *Fred Holder* |
| Segmented Turning: A Complete Guide | *Ron Hampton* |
| Turned Boxes: 50 Designs | *Chris Stott* |
| Turning Green Wood | *Michael O'Donnell* |
| Turning Pens and Pencils | *Kip Christensen & Rex Burningham* |
| Woodturning: Forms and Materials | *John Hunnex* |
| Woodturning: A Foundation Course (New Edition) | *Keith Rowley* |
| Woodturning: A Fresh Approach | *Robert Chapman* |
| Woodturning: An Individual Approach | *Dave Regester* |
| Woodturning: A Source Book of Shapes | *John Hunnex* |
| Woodturning Masterclass | *Tony Boase* |
| Woodturning Techniques | *GMC Publications* |

### WOODWORKING

| | |
|---|---|
| Beginning Picture Marquetry | *Lawrence Threadgold* |
| Celtic Carved Lovespoons: 30 Patterns | *Sharon Littley & Clive Griffin* |
| Celtic Woodcraft | *Glenda Bennett* |
| Complete Woodfinishing (Revised Edition) | *Ian Hosker* |
| David Charlesworth's Furniture-Making | |
| Techniques | *David Charlesworth* |
| David Charlesworth's Furniture-Making Techniques – Volume 2 | |
| | *David Charlesworth* |
| Furniture-Making Projects for the | |
| Wood Craftsman | *GMC Publications* |
| Furniture-Making Techniques for the | |
| Wood Craftsman | *GMC Publications* |
| Furniture Projects with the Router | *Kevin Ley* |
| Furniture Restoration (Practical Crafts) | *Kevin Jan Bonner* |
| Furniture Restoration: A Professional at Work | *John Lloyd* |
| Furniture Restoration and Repair for Beginners | *Kevin Jan Bonner* |
| Furniture Restoration Workshop | *Kevin Jan Bonner* |
| Green Woodwork | *Mike Abbott* |
| Intarsia: 30 Patterns for the Scrollsaw | *John Everett* |
| Kevin Ley's Furniture Projects | *Kevin Ley* |
| Making Chairs and Tables – Volume 2 | *GMC Publications* |

| | |
|---|---|
| Making Classic English Furniture | *Paul Richardson* |
| Making Heirloom Boxes | *Peter Lloyd* |
| Making Screw Threads in Wood | *Fred Holder* |
| Making Woodwork Aids and Devices | *Robert Wearing* |
| Mastering the Router | *Ron Fox* |
| Pine Furniture Projects for the Home | *Dave Mackenzie* |
| Router Magic: Jigs, Fixtures and Tricks to | |
| Unleash your Router's Full Potential | *Bill Hylton* |
| Router Projects for the Home | *GMC Publications* |
| Router Tips & Techniques | *Robert Wearing* |
| Routing: A Workshop Handbook | *Anthony Bailey* |
| Routing for Beginners | *Anthony Bailey* |
| Sharpening: The Complete Guide | *Jim Kingshott* |
| Space-Saving Furniture Projects | *Dave Mackenzie* |
| Stickmaking: A Complete Course | *Andrew Jones & Clive George* |
| Stickmaking Handbook | *Andrew Jones & Clive George* |
| Storage Projects for the Router | *GMC Publications* |
| Veneering: A Complete Course | *Ian Hosker* |
| Veneering Handbook | *Ian Hosker* |
| Woodworking Techniques and Projects | *Anthony Bailey* |
| Woodworking with the Router: Professional | |
| Router Techniques any Woodworker can Use | |
| | *Bill Hylton & Fred Matlack* |

### UPHOLSTERY

| | |
|---|---|
| Upholstery: A Complete Course (Revised Edition) | *David James* |
| Upholstery Restoration | *David James* |
| Upholstery Techniques & Projects | *David James* |
| Upholstery Tips and Hints | *David James* |

### TOY MAKING

| | |
|---|---|
| Scrollsaw Toy Projects | *Ivor Carlyle* |
| Scrollsaw Toys for All Ages | *Ivor Carlyle* |

### DOLLS' HOUSES AND MINIATURES

| | |
|---|---|
| 1/12 Scale Character Figures for the Dolls' House | *James Carrington* |
| Americana in 1/12 Scale: 50 Authentic Projects | |
| | *Joanne Ogreenc & Mary Lou Santovec* |
| The Authentic Georgian Dolls' House | *Brian Long* |
| A Beginners' Guide to the Dolls' House Hobby | *Jean Nisbett* |
| Celtic, Medieval and Tudor Wall Hangings in | |
| 1/12 Scale Needlepoint | *Sandra Whitehead* |
| Creating Decorative Fabrics: Projects in 1/12 Scale | *Janet Storey* |
| Dolls' House Accessories, Fixtures and Fittings | *Andrea Barham* |
| Dolls' House Furniture: | |
| Easy-to-Make Projects in 1/12 Scale | *Freida Gray* |
| Dolls' House Makeovers | *Jean Nisbett* |
| Dolls' House Window Treatments | *Eve Harwood* |
| Edwardian-Style Hand-Knitted Fashion for 1/12 Scale Dolls | |
| | *Yvonne Wakefield* |
| How to Make Your Dolls' House Special: Fresh Ideas for Decorating | |
| | *Beryl Armstrong* |
| Making 1/12 Scale Wicker Furniture | |
| for the Dolls' House | *Sheila Smith* |
| Making Miniature Chinese Rugs and Carpets | *Carol Phillipson* |
| Making Miniature Food and Market Stalls | *Angie Scarr* |
| Making Miniature Gardens | *Freida Gray* |
| Making Miniature Oriental | |
| Rugs & Carpets | *Meik & Ian McNaughton* |
| Making Miniatures: Projects for the | |
| 1/12 Scale Dolls' House | *Christiane Berridge* |
| Making Period Dolls' House Accessories | *Andrea Barham* |
| Making Tudor Dolls' Houses | *Derek Rowbottom* |
| Making Upholstered Furniture in 1/12 Scale | *Janet Storey* |
| Making Victorian Dolls' House Furniture | *Patricia King* |
| Medieval and Tudor Needlecraft: | |
| Knights and Ladies in 1/12 Scale | *Sandra Whitehead* |

# MAGAZINES

WOODTURNING • WOODCARVING • FURNITURE & CABINETMAKING • THE ROUTER • NEW WOODWORKING
THE DOLLS' HOUSE MAGAZINE • OUTDOOR PHOTOGRAPHY • TRAVEL PHOTOGRAPHY
BLACK & WHITE PHOTOGRAPHY • MACHINE KNITTING NEWS • KNITTING
GUILD OF MASTER CRAFTSMEN NEWS

The above represents only a selection of titles currently published or scheduled to be published. All are available direct from the Publishers
or through bookshops, newsagents and specialist retailers. To place an order, or to obtain a complete catalogue, contact:

**GMC PUBLICATIONS, CASTLE PLACE, 166 HIGH STREET, LEWES,
EAST SUSSEX BN7 1XU UNITED KINGDOM
TEL: 01273 488005  FAX: 01273 478606  e-mail: pubs@thegmcgroup.com**

Orders by credit card are accepted

NOV - - 2019